THE PEACEMONGERS

ROBERT DUNCAN CULVER

THE PEACE-MONGERS

Tyndale House Publishers, Inc.
Wheaton, Illinois

To Celeste:

nurse, typist,
manuscript critic,
and loving wife

Unless otherwise indicated, Bible quotations are taken from the King James Version. Other quotations are taken from the Revised Standard Version (RSV) © 1946, 1952 by the Division of Christian Education of the National Council of Churches of Christ in the United States of America.

First printing, May 1985

Library of Congress Catalog Card Number 84-52668
ISBN 0-8423-4789-5, paper

Printed in the United States of America

CONTENTS

PREFACE

The Bible gives little support to the fond hope that the horrors of war will soon cease on the face of our green planet. The angel Gabriel said to the prophet Daniel: ". . . to the end there shall be war" (Dan. 9:26, RSV). Jesus used one of his last moments with his disciples to say of the coming Christian epoch, "You will hear of wars and rumors of wars" (Matt. 24:6, RSV). The last book of the Bible pictures four dreadful horsemen sent forth by Providence to introduce the consummation of human affairs. The second rides a red horse with power "to take peace from the earth, and that they should kill one another: and there was given unto him a great sword" (Rev. 6:4).

The reason for war is not hard to find. James states it plainly: "What causes wars, and what causes fightings among you? Is it not your passions that are at war in your members? You desire and do not have; so you kill. And you covet and cannot obtain; so you fight and wage war" (James 4:1, 2, RSV).

War is not, then, a problem peculiar to the present generation or century. Although there have been epochs of relative peace among nations (the nineteenth century was such a time), war never has ceased to threaten the nations of earth. "The noiseless tenor of their way" of Thomas Gray's famous elegy is and has been for most of earth's inhabitants throughout history an ideal rather than a fact. Disturbers of the peace never cease to threaten.

Nearly forty years after the close of the greatest of all wars (1939–45) everybody is keenly aware of wars and threats of them. The media are full of news and editorializing about them. The tone of discussion has moved in waves from pianissimo to fortissimo several times within this period, depending on the latest moods of the movers of public opinion. And the threats can never be ignored.

I was raised in a "peace church." It was not pacifist, as Quakers are, but it nonetheless espoused nonresistance, following the usual doctrine of European pietism. I mention this to inform the reader that I have not come lately to the subject. For me it was staple diet in sermons, church resolutions, conference discussions, and the like from the beginning. The matter was always presented in dead earnest, with sincere effort to be as biblical as possible.

The peace churches have lately begun to march with the times, along with everyone else, in spite of themselves. Some of these churches continue to move along the wholesome line of their historic loyalty to Christian evangelical orthodoxy. Others, however, are veering toward the perilous track of doctrinal liberalism and a special kind of social activism. A new kind of pacifism bearing small inner resemblance to their historic nonresistance is being used to lead them astray. This is part of what this book is about.

The Second World War was several years in the future when as a high school sophomore I made a first attempt to preach a sermon. That great war was soon to end when I made my maiden lecture on theology in a theological seminary. The times since then have compelled me to continue reading, thinking, preaching, and writing about war and whether or not it can ever be justified, and about whether it is right or wrong for Christians to join battle as combatants. This book on Christian doctrine regarding war must be something safe for my six grandsons to read, if they should happen to want my advice. It will be partly history, partly doctrine, and certainly partly recall of a spiritual pilgrimage.

PART ONE
Past Pacifism

CHAPTER 1
TO WAR OR NOT TO WAR?

If we know anything at all about the Bible, we know that Jesus said many things in praise of peacemaking. The Sermon on the Mount speaks of this in vigorous language: turn the other cheek, go a second mile, agree with your adversary quickly, and so on. Our Lord was a man of peace. As far as we know, he never lifted a hand against any man except when he cleared "my Father's house"—the temple—with some sort of impassioned demonstration if not actual physical force. Later, writers of the New Testament held his behavior before Christians as example for them: "Christ also suffered for us, leaving us an example" (1 Pet. 2:21).

This sort of counsel, however, is not unique to Jesus. From beginning to end the Bible teaches that personal vengeance is always wrong. The principle of "an eye for an eye and a tooth for a tooth" is stated four or five times in the Bible. But it is only a metaphorical way of requiring that, in the public administration of civil law, penalties should always be in just proportion to offenses committed—i.e., the magistrate should extract no more than the value of one tooth or one eye from an offender who has done injury equal to that amount. The very law of Moses, which first states the principle, also makes clear that all vengeance is the Lord's, for "the Lord will vindicate his people" (Deut. 32:36, RSV). Romans 12:17–21 is a melding of Old Testament passages on the subject: "Recompense no man evil for evil . . . Avenge not yourselves . . . Vengeance is mine: I will repay, saith the Lord [See Deut. 32:35]. Therefore if thine enemy hunger, feed him; if he thirst, give him drink: for in so doing thou shalt heap coals of fire on his head. Be not overcome of evil, but overcome evil with good" [See also Prov. 25:21, 22]. There are many other passages such as these.

Therefore, a sensitive Christian will be cautious about personal use of coercive force of any kind. He knows that children require forcible control, as many of the Proverbs enjoin, but beyond that, even indirect coercion—such as threats or manipulation—must be used with caution.

But does this mean that all worshippers of God in Christ are forbidden to use force in assisting civil government administer public law—civil and criminal? Have we nothing to do with apprehending criminals or jailing, trying, and punishing them? Must other people who are not Christians perform these unpleasant and even dangerous duties very necessary to maintenance of the civil peace (1 Tim. 2:1–3), which we all enjoy and for which we are commanded to pray? How about wars of national defense and public policy? Do Christians have duties toward them? If so, what? If not, why?

The clear teaching of the Bible, seldom challenged by any serious interpreters, is that rulers have the right to levy and collect taxes, to pass laws, to compel civil obedience, and to punish disobedience. Caesar has his "things" and Pilate has civil power "given from above." Rulers are "ministers of God"; they rightly "bear the sword," the instrument of law-enforcement, of war, and of death penalties, for the magistrate is a "revenger to execute wrath on him that doeth evil." Paul accepted capital punishment as appropriate punishment for capital crimes, for he asserted willingness to accept judicial execution if guilty of a crime "worthy of death." Obedience to laws and rulers is necessary, he says, not only for fear of punishment but for good conscience. It is not enough to have "fear of God"; we must also "honor the king." See Acts 25:11; Rom. 13:1–7; Titus 3:1; 1 Pet. 2:13–17; John 19:11; Matt. 22:15–22.

Though warm love of country is normal for Christians, these provisions of scripture do not necessarily produce flag-waving fanatics. For though they are "God's ministers," rulers are known to unjustly imprison and slay holy prophets and apostles. They sometimes exile other Christians for the word of God and the testimony of Jesus. Although they are divinely authorized supporters of public weal and peaceful social order, magistrates sometimes misuse their power through malice or ignorance. See Rom. 13:3; Acts 5:17; 12:1–19; Rev. 1:9; Matt. 10:16–19. Hamlet's famous soliloquy has memorialized the oppressor's wrong, the proud man's contumely, and the law's delay. Justice is frequently miscarried, yet it is effected by civil government regularly enough that the scriptures say rulers are "not a terror to good works but to the evil."

Rulers are not always admirable. They are often ignorant, ruthless and mean (Pilate, Herod); clever (Galleo); weak (Agrippa); indecisive (Felix, Festus); or even bloodthirsty (Nero). Paul says few of them are among God's elect; none of "the princes of this world" of Jesus' day understood the divine wisdom, "for if they had [known it], they would not have crucified the Lord of glory" (1 Cor. 2:8ff.; 1:26; Acts 4:25–28).

There results, then, a kind of dialectic—a problem of reconciling, or of deciding what to do about a good that is also an evil. Every Christian must be involved to some degree with civil government, from the time his name is recorded in the register of births at county or state offices until he signs up for the draft, pays his real estate taxes, or enlists for military duty. At most of these stages he has some sort of decision to make: he cannot get along *without* government, but how far should he go *with* it?

In the areas that count most, Christians have always responded favorably to government. They ought to be, and actually are, the most law-abiding and country-loving people. As long as their consciences are not offended by what government requires, they are quick to support it. The lives of the first missionaries (Paul, for example) were protected from Jewish fanatics and heathen mobs by the magistrates and police, even though sometimes government ignorantly persecuted them. Only when convinced that to obey God they had to disobey man did they behave differently.

Sometimes government has made Christians the object of persecution or unjust discrimination. The last years of Paul's life, when he was imprisoned and then executed by the Roman government, were such a time. The Christians of the USSR have been living under such a regime for more than sixty years, and the Chinese Christians for nearly forty years.

Under these circumstances it is not surprising that many Christians have felt they could not conscientiously fight for their countries. There is a long record of what we call conscientious objection on biblical grounds, and our century has had its share of it. Later we will try to trace the history of conscientious objection and Christian pacifism. It will then be necessary to define these terms. For now we will simply observe that many Christians throughout history have refused to bear arms. Some of them have even condemned their governments for resorting to war. Certain Protestant denominations have such teachings as part of their basic affirmations of faith. These denominations are often called the "peace churches."

Shortly after World War II the World Council of Churches was formed. Many of its leaders heralded that the peace churches were pointing the way for world Christianity. These leaders sought to get the basic documents of the World Council to include a declaration that war is not only a social evil but a sin. Largely through the vigorous influence of Reinhold Niebuhr, author and professor at Union Theological Seminary in New York, the effort failed. At that time there were painfully fresh memories of the war and the frightful destruction of two Japanese cities by the American atomic bomb. It was the heyday of what has come to be called nuclear pacifism. There was quite a volume of pacifist literature at the time—secular, peace-church, and other.

Anyone who grew up as I did in the years between the two world wars may remember that Sunday school papers and quarterlies advocated pacifism nearly as vociferously as they advocated temperance. Even before that, the optimistic temper of the late nineteenth century led many church people to predict the twentieth century would be "The Christian Century." A new magazine for liberal Protestants, still published, was named just that. In spite of the Great War (1914–18) the notion persisted. The new League of Nations, the World Court at The Hague, and especially the Kellogg-Briand Treaty (Paris Pact) of 1929 were to help insure that the Great War was to be "the war to end war."

I distinctly remember hearing my teachers in public school say these things in 1929. The public breathed the atmosphere of expectation of perpetual peace. I also remember hearing people argue against these notions in Sunday school. There will be no world peace, they said, until the second coming of Christ. But they were not being heard in either the governmental or ecclesiastical seats of power. Communication between religious liberals and conservatives in those days seldom took place, so the latter did not learn for decades that even the liberals were slowly giving up their utopian hopes. The optimism was shattered, not by any fundamentalist objections, true though they may have been, but by blows from several other quarters.

The first blow was theological. During the 1920s the powerful voice of Karl Barth overwhelmed the liberal, optimistic theology of the Europeans with a doctrine of man's inborn depravity. Reinhold Niebuhr, with similar arguments, handily disposed of the shallow, liberal optimism in America with his powerful writings (beginning with *Moral Man and Immoral Society*, 1932), lectures, and sermons. At that time no theologian of the liberal establishment successfully challenged Barthianism or Niebuhr's new orthodoxy. Roland Bainton wrote, "Karl Barth in Europe revived the Calvinist picture of human nature, and Hitler arose to illustrate it."[1]

Bainton's remark relates also to the second blow, a political one. Coming to power in 1933, Hitler proceeded to scare the pacific politicians of Europe to impotence. When Neville Chamberlain, England's prime minister, signed an agreement with Hitler at Munich in 1938, the timid policy of appeasement was put in place to preserve "peace in our time." People were divided over Chamberlain's action. My own mother said to me and to my greatly exasperated father, "I think he did the right thing." But World War II broke out the next year.

The third blow was economic—the Great Depression of the 30s led to social upheaval around the world. The fourth blow was military—with increasing armaments in several quarters (especially Germany and Japan) and a terrible civil war in Spain during the middle 30s, World War II loomed on the horizon.

Universal fear of war, inspired by the most bloody war in human history, made the founding of the United Nations inevitable. Young people today can hardly imagine the universal popular demand for it. Americans were undecided about whether to be ashamed or proud or simply thankful for what happened when America dropped atomic bombs on two Japanese cities. All were then horrified and remain so.

Earlier, President Woodrow Wilson couldn't get the Senate to vote the U.S.A. into the League of Nations, but a generation later I think most Americans—at least including my theology teachers—thought we had to support the United Nations. Even if a pessimistic eschatology said it wouldn't work, we had to try it. One united world—if not Christ's then the Antichrist's—seemed better than the perils of nuclear wars. The slogan "One World" was used by a Republican presidential candidate even before the war's end. For nearly forty years many people have been saying that thermonuclear weapons now make the idea of justified war obsolete. Perhaps all of us who have lived through these years as adults have felt this way at some time or other.

Several denominations of Christians have insisted it is wrong for Christians to have anything to do with bearing arms as police or as soldiers. Mennonites, Brethren (Dunkers), and Quakers—in America since colonial times—have always reminded us that they take this view of matters. While not agreeing in every detail, they believe that all forms of physical coercion are wrong for Christians. Some—such as the "Defenseless Mennonites"—even hold that it is wrong for Christians to call upon police for physical protection. The example of Jesus, the Sermon on the Mount, and similar scripture passages are cited. The Old Testament wars of God's people are explained as being against God's will. They reason that if the Israelites had trusted God, they would not have had to fight wars. God would have defended them, or if not, then it would have been better to suffer and die. We must examine these views further.

Most Christian leaders have taught differently. When Jesus spoke of turning the other cheek, going the second mile, suffering for righteousness' sake, and nonresistance to evil, he had in mind the personal behavior of Christians as persons. These sayings were not addressed to governments or to the actions of government officers in enforcing laws about contracts of purchase, deeds of ownership, and the like, where coercive force must be wielded by government to make the laws work. Neither was Jesus speaking of how Christians who happen to be clerks of court, sheriffs, or police officers should behave in official capacity. Jesus' short, pithy sayings are similar to the proverbs of the Old Testament. Like them they contain many figures of speech—simile, metaphor, hyperbole, and others. Christ's literal meaning must be sought in the figures he used—as in all such language.

For example, Jesus spoke of how one must hate one's parents if he is to follow the Lord. Jesus simply meant we should not prefer parents' claims; he did not mean we should literally hate them. The Sermon on the Mount was never intended as a manual for magistrates in conduct of public affairs.

Civil government, as Reformation theology interprets the Bible, was instituted by God after the Flood (Gen. 8, 9). Those who shed man's blood shall have their blood shed by man collectively (the government). Those who take a sword *unlawfully,* as Peter did, shall perish by the sword *lawfully.* God specifically forbids us personal, coercive power over our violence-prone neighbors (Rom. 12), but he provides us protection from the violent neighbor and restraint of the outlaw through public law and government agencies such as police and courts (Rom. 13). Most Christians do not hesitate to call the police if threatened by burglars or by other forms of unlawful attack. Most churches expect police protection—however imperfect—for their chapels, schools, parsonages, and the like. It seldom occurs to them that it might be wrong or unchristian to be a policeman or soldier or judge, if occasion should arise. They vote, run for office, and serve in departments of government and its military departments in all good conscience.

Religious pacifism, if we may now use the term, does not seem to be a necessary inference or direction of the Bible to a majority of Christian believers. If the Bible neither commands nor forbids Christians to bear arms, then other grounds will necessarily have to be found for whatever one decides to do. Christians in each period will make up their minds in different ways and for different reasons. A brief history of Christian attitudes toward war and military service now claims our attention.

CHAPTER 2
NONRESISTANCE IN THE EARLY CHURCH

All the persons whose names and history are told in the New Testament lived within the Roman Empire. Nearly all who dwelt in the Empire were conquered peoples. They had little to say about how civil affairs should be run and much to gain simply by tending to their own business. Only a few were citizens (Paul was one). There were different levels of civil status in every community, from outright slavery to full civil status, but since most residents of the Empire were mere subjects, only a few had full rights and liberties. Armies were Roman and professional, consisting almost entirely of mercenaries. These armies policed the Empire and kept peace over western and southern Europe, much of the Near East, and northern Africa. Residents of the Roman Empire enjoyed the benefits of relative peace in the world.

When the Jews of Palestine rebelled against Rome and brought on the destructive war and devastation of A.D. 70, the Christians simply moved out of the line of fire. They would have nothing of it.

Paul was protected by Roman police, who several times saved his life. He traveled everywhere without need of visas or passports. The great missionary apostle was proud of his Roman citizenship, acknowledging that Rome's power was "of God," that its laws and magistrates were a "terror to evil works," not to good ones, and encouraged payment of taxes and obedience to officials of the Roman state. At the end he apparently willingly accepted the unjust judgment of the courts and execution.

Christians of the New Testament reports were not asked to become soldiers. The New Testament says nothing directly about whether Christians should or should not enter military professions. We are not told that any were advised by Jesus or an apostle to get out of military life.

At any rate, the Roman state—which at first protected Christians—after three or four decades saw a challenge to its "lordship" among the now numerous believers, most of whom would gladly obey their rulers and pay taxes, but would not join in pagan religious rites prescribed by official state religion. Caesar also saw some kind of challenge to his rule or person when they confessed in church that "Jesus Christ is Lord" but would not make a religious confession in court or in the army that Caesar was Lord. The early Christians did not refuse to acknowledge that in matters of worldly life and civil law, Caesar was indeed their lord.

Such was the situation of the Christians of the Empire of Rome almost as long as it lasted (until A.D. 315, when an emperor granted official toleration for Christianity).

Because of their circumstances, it is not surprising that the first generations of Christians refused to participate in military service. Many scholars have sifted through the historical evidence, some with friendly approval of what the Christians did about war and some with disagreement or disapproval, but there is not much disagreement about the facts. It is generally acknowledged that until the Christianizing of the Empire's government in the fourth century there was slight, though increasing, involvement of Christians in the armies of Rome: "From the end of the New Testament period to the decade 170–180 there is no evidence whatever of Christians in the army."[1] It is quite clear that "prior to about A.D. 174 it is impossible to speak of Christian soldiers."[2] About this time the famous heretic Celsus reproached Christians for failing to help defend the Empire, charging, "If all men were to do the same as you, there would be nothing to prevent the king from being left in utter solitude and desertion and the forces of the Empire would fall into the hands of the wildest and most lawless barbarians."[3] There is no evidence that any of the Christian leaders in the early pre-Constantinian era approved a military career as right for a believer in Jesus Christ. Extant writings are not plain in every respect, but their tenor is clearly nonresistant, if not technically pacifist. Guy Franklin Herschberger cites convincing passages from the *Didache* and from Polycarp, Justin Martyr, and Athenagoras.[4]

From A.D. 180 until 313, when Christianity became legal, it must be said that "all of the outstanding writers of the East and West repudiated participation in warfare for Christians."[5] Military service came to be regarded by some (the Canons of Hypollytus are cited) as admissible if bearing of arms was not part of the service. This allowed Christians to enter some orders of police, or to be firemen. They could hire out to transport, postal service, ordnance, secretarial service, and other forms of noncombatant government work. (Tertullian, the usual rigorist, disagreed that Christians should become involved even in noncombatant government service.)

In the year 312–313 the Roman emperor made Christianity a legal religion; official persecution ceased. After that, Christian objections to participating in military defense of the Empire declined. Eventually, objections to military service on religious grounds came to be regarded by Christians as treasonous.

From that day to this, most Christian writers who have treated the subject of the Christian and civil government have regarded the protection of the free worship of Christians as the God-given duty of their civil governors. Today pious judges, military officers, police officers in uniform are frequently given honorable position in Christian assemblies, sometimes addressing them.

Objections on principle to Christians' being magistrates, police officers, and military personnel have been by a minority. Up until fairly recently this minority has been almost exclusively a profoundly religious group, people moved by strongly-held moral convictions based on sincerely-believed doctrines. They have been convinced that they were following clear biblical teachings. Being a minority, and not infrequently a socially self-isolated group, they have often been misunderstood and sometimes have been mistreated by other Christians.

Scholars have searched the writings of the early church to find out what reasons the early Christians gave for their near uniform rejection of military service. Today there is general agreement on the facts. The early Christians developed some of their views simply in reaction to the fact that the government under which they lived would periodically persecute and execute them for no other reason than that they were Christians. Some of their views they based on what they esteemed to be clear biblical teaching; other views are reasoned answers to charges and criticism. The reasons the Christians gave for refusing to be a part of the emperor's military forces may be reduced to six.

1. They believed participation in war to be completely incompatible with the commands and example of Christ. They emphasized the parts of the New Testament that are of the same tenor. Tertullian asked, "If we are enjoined to love our enemies, whom are we to hate? If injured we are forbidden to retaliate. Who then can suffer injury at our hand?"[6] Clement of Alexandria and Cyprian are frequently quoted to similar effect. This remains today the most respectable reason, the one which requires that Christian conscientious objection should be given honorable treatment by all men, whether in agreement or not. There can be no higher motive or argument. Many loyal Christians believe this way. In a sense, this has always been the only important reason for what is sometimes called biblical pacifism.

2. Origen stated another reason: Christians by their prayers and disciplined lives are of more use to kings than are soldiers. In time of war, he said, Christians contribute more to the common weal of the country by continuing peaceful pursuits than they would by going to war. The Christians of the time felt that their country's chief foes, like their own, were spiritual, not carnal: that spiritual weapons such as preaching and prayer and the practice of piety were the weapons most likely to produce constructive results. The Epistle to Diognetus, an early Christian document, states this in a different way: "What the soul of a man is to his body the Christians are to the world, ordering, instructing, guiding it."[7]

3. The third reason was a rather poignant, ironic one. Before the persecutions ceased, Christians could remind themselves that they suffered at the emperor's hand whether they joined his armies or not. Why should they fight to defend a government that entertained the populace by throwing Christians to the beasts in the colosseum? The government of Rome might be their only worldly protection against thieves and wanton criminals, but Rome was also their chronic enemy. In that strange world some of the most upright pagans conceived their moral duty to be the suppression or extermination of religious dissent. This was true of some of Rome's least corrupt emperors and territorial administrators.

4. Near the end of the pre-Constantinian period the Christians became numerous enough that they might possibly have defended themselves successfully against their persecutors, but did not do so because they expected vindication in the world to come. "All Christians placed their citizenship in heaven. On earth they were but pilgrims and strangers. A reason definitely assigned for their unwillingness, despite their numbers, to take up arms against their persecutors is the certainty of their vindication in the life to come."[8] (See note on page 26 regarding Tertullian's defense of the ancient Christians' way of life.) Even at the end of the Empire, Roman citizenship did not come automatically by being born in a province of the Empire. Millions of residents in the various provinces, descendents of generations of residents, were without status or rights. Thus the only citizenship most of the earliest generations of believers had was in heaven—there was no talk of being citizens of two realms, as we hear so much about today.

5. Another reason had to do with the requirement that soldiers engage in idolatry. Any government office involved some compromise with idolatry. The privilege of citizenship theoretically required participation in the state religion. Indeed, mere residence made accommodation with idolatrous rites obligatory if local magistrates were vigorous in enforcing Roman laws. Exposure to danger from this quarter was even worse in the army, where image-worship and offering of incense to a god or the emperor were part of the regular regimen. Many died martyrs' deaths whenever idol-worship

was enforced. Noncombatant military service was hardly less dangerous to the man who refused to burn incense to the emperor. "The cult of the deified emperor was particularly prevalent in the camps. Officers were called upon to sacrifice; privates participated at least by their attendance. Origen listed idolatry and robbery as sins common in the army."[9]

Several modern writers (Bethune Baker, Ernst Troeltsch, Paul Ramsey) have suggested that this is the main reason why early Christians refused to enter military service. They argue that if this is so, then the precedent set has no bearing upon Christian ethics of war today, for idolatry is no part of modern military service.[10]

6. It has been asserted, perhaps with some justification, that all Christians in the earliest years and in the more primitive sects, refused military service because they thought the coming of the Lord was near. They believed the Lord would soon destroy the very Empire they were called upon to defend if they entered military service. (Perhaps it is true that, after Constantine, they tended to depend more on the emperor than on the Lord, with the result that they were more willing to support the emperor's wars.)

These were the reasons. Were they adequate? Was their interpretation of scripture correct? If it was praiseworthy for them to practice pacifism, is it incumbent on believers of every age and nation to do the same?

The views of prominent Christian leaders of those early centuries on some other questions are rejected by many informed believers today: the developing legalism, dependence on rites—called sacraments for salvation (sacerdotalism), and the transfer of all liturgical acts and church government to a priestly class (prelacy). Few today would accept Tertullian's eschatology or Cyprian's incipient papalism. For now we only raise the question: Are the early Christians' reasons for withdrawal from military service and essential social separation valid for Christians today?

Before we leave consideration of the views of the early church regarding Roman government and its wars, we must pause to pay our respects. No age of mankind is ever in a good position to pass just judgment on an earlier one. The situation today is very different from theirs. We bring our own experiences and picture of world-reality to theirs, and they are not quite commensurate. Their world had not been modified from immemorial heathenism, as Western civilization now has been. That world was hopelessly corrupt. The Roman government did a fair job of preserving civil order, but even that began to break down, finally failing altogether. It was already falling apart by the fourth century. Tertullian, the period's most articulate writer on the theme of the Christian and government, asserted that apart from prayer, witness, good example, and deeds of charity, there was little else Christians could do in and for society. They were, in the eyes of their world, not good enough to have any part in it at all. They were regarded as simply and fully "out of step" at almost every point. They were magnificent in purity and in successful witness. Modern orthodox Mennonite writers cite many cases where officers of the Roman army became converted to Christianity and thereupon gave up their weapons and resigned. Usually they were put to death for this alleged disloyalty. Who can fault faith like that? No wonder the numbers of Christians increased.

As I assess their reasons for social separation and for nonresistance leading to martyrdom by the thousands, I have to ask myself, Who am I to judge them? They were not perfect. But neither are we.

Contrariwise, in the practical matter of participation or nonparticipation in wars of defense and other presumably justified military activity, their reasons and motives are only partially applicable in Western countries, though for Christians under communism, the situations are remarkably parallel. We in America do not have to pour out libations or burn incense to a deified emperor; there is no literal idolatry required in the army (though Jehovah's Witnesses think there is); our government does not entertain our unemployed by pitting us against tigers in a colosseum; we can pray for our country in or out of the army. As to Christ's teaching and example, we shall seek to demonstrate that they do not require of believers to renounce all use of physical force under lawful conditions nor the sort of social separation upon which Anabaptist groups have historically insisted. In other words, while we cannot ignore their bright example, the decision of the early Christians is not *per se* decisive for us.[11]

APPENDIX
Tertullian's *Apologetics*

Page after page of Tertullian's great *Apologetics* states the themes of several of the early Christians' arguments for nonparticipation in the military. Following are two samples of Tertullian's vivid, inimitable style. They are from his *Apology, DeSpectaculis,* trans. T. R. Glover, Loeb Classical Library, No. 250 (Cambridge: Harvard University Press, 1966).

> *If as we have said above, we are bidden love our enemies, whom have we to hate? Again, if, when a man injures us we are forbidden to retaliate, that the action may not make us alike, whom then can we injure? Look at this, yourselves, and think it over! How often do you wreak your fury on the Christians, in part obeying your own instincts, in part the laws? How often, too, without regard to you, does the unfriendly mob on its own account assail us with stones and fire. [According to Tertullian, the mobs even desecrated Christian burials.] Yet I ask though Christians are so sworn to one purpose, so ready for death itself, what retaliation for injury can you charge against us, though a single night and a few little torches could work a lavish revenge, if among us wrong might be wiped out with wrong? But away with such a thought that God's school [Christians] should either avenge itself with man's fire, or resent the suffering that is its probation. (XXXVII, 1–3)*

> *I will now show you the proceedings with which the Christian association occupies itself; I have proved they are not wrong, so now I will make you see they are good. We are a society [corpus] with a common religious feeling, unity of discipline, a common bond of hope. We meet in gather-*

ing and congregation to approach God in prayer, massing our forces to surround Him. This violence that we do Him pleases God. (Tertullian ironically contrasts Roman mobs with the Christians' orderly assemblies.) We pray also for Emperors, for their ministers and those in authority, for the security of the world, for peace on earth, for postponement of the end. We meet to read the books of God—if anything in the nature of the times bids us look to the future or open our eyes to facts. In any case, with those holy words we feed our faith, we lift up our hope, we confirm our confidence; and no less we reinforce our teaching by inculcation of God's precepts. There is, besides, exhortation in our gatherings, rebuke, divine censure. For judgment is passed, and it carries great weight, as it must among men certain that God sees them; and it is a notable foretaste of judgment to come, if any man has so sinned as to be banished from all share in our prayer, our assembly, and all holy intercourse. Our presidents are elders of proven character, men who have reached this honor not for a price, but by character, for nothing that is God's goes for a price. (XXXIX, 1–4)

Tertullian proceeds to describe a monthly voluntary collection of money used to feed or bury the poor, orphans, old slaves, shipwrecked mariners, miners (slaves), and prisoners, "provided that it is for the sake of God's school, become the pensioners of their confession."

CHAPTER 3
DENIZENS OF THE EMPIRE

From the end of the Roman persecution (A.D. 315) until the beginning of the Reformation (1517), most Christians, at least the ones we know much about, were within boundaries of the largest extension of the Roman Empire. From the beginning of the Empire, there were two main variations of the common cultures: eastern and western. These divisions became defined geographically by Constantine, each with a capital city—Constantinople (now Istanbul, Turkey) in the East and Rome in the West. Greek continued as the chief language in the East and Latin became the main language of the West. Though always conscious that they were all of one universal (catholic, ecumenical) church, two distinct kinds of Christianity developed.

In the West the Roman government broke down within a century and a half of the edict of toleration (A.D. 315). Before long, such civil order as existed was in the hands of a great variety of self-appointed lords ruling over innumerable small areas. The Christian bishop of the ancient capital, Rome, was called the pope. With an episcopal hierarchy under his leadership, he gave Europe the only sort of unity—civil or otherwise—it possessed. The ancient tradition of a world empire centered at Rome gave the pope great prestige and much power to enforce such general order as could be achieved.

At the very period when the church became a tolerated religion and then the only legal one, the form and tradition of a unified Roman world was already breaking up. It had been the hope of the emperor that Christianity might assist against the disintegration.

In the East the Empire continued for another millenium. The long line of emperors of the East all reigned from Constantinople. The Greeks, as they were called, resisted encroachment by Persians, Arabs, Turks, and others with varying success, though with gradual loss of territory until Constantinople was conquered by the Turkish armies in 1453.

Before the Empire quite fully divided into a disintegrated West and a shrinking East, there was a change in the attitude of Christians toward the wars of their "world." We know little of what the common people believed, but we know that leading Christian authors—some with much reservation, some with none—now could look upon their governments and their wars with a friendly eye. A complete analysis and description of these developments would take too much space here.[1]

We may generalize by saying that the attitudes that had prevailed for centuries rapidly solidified as soon as Christians were allowed the legal right to live with the normal privileges of other residents of the Empire. In the West these attitudes were informally shaped by bits and pieces by many preachers, prelates, and writers. They addressed their teachings to Christian laymen in civil office. Among the most influential were Ambrose of Milan and Augustine of Hippo. I think it is too much to say that they in their generations gave Christians the so-called just war theory. It is true, however, that they expressed what quickly became the common Christian view: Christians may in good conscience participate in all the functions and offices that scripture assigns to civil government; conduct of war for adequate reasons of state is one of those functions. In all this they knew they had to remain Christians, but they realized that the taking of the life of man by man in war is not murder. Probably few of the Christians of that transitional epoch even knew the names of Ambrose and Augustine, but as far as we can tell from the present distance in time, almost all took this view of matters.

Ordained clergy, monks, and others whose "vocations" were of the religious order were not supposed to fight in wars. Most of the land's inhabitants (citizens hardly is the word) could not be warriors even if they wished; after things settled into the pattern familiar to us as feudalism, military action was ordinarily carried out by professional upper-class soldiers. An exception was the mass armies of the Crusades during the eleventh–thirteenth centuries. Noncombatants (most of the population) were supposed to be left unharmed. In that violent age, Christianity, through the common sentiment of the church expressed by popes, bishops, preachers, and a few theological writers, sought to reduce the brutality of war, and with some success. In the East the emperor was head of one unitary state, including church and its bishops (Caesaropapism). There the church was reduced to a department of the state with no power over wars other than to support the emperor. In such a situation there may have been multitudes of Christians in and out of armies who followed conscience to nonresistance conclusions and died as passive sufferers. Many fled the Empire. We know them as Assyrians, Nestorians, and Copts, among others. As far as we can determine, however, they were not doctrinaire pacifists, however pacific in manners of living.

As for the West, we know only a little of the dissident Christians. The Cathari, Albigensians, Waldensians, Hussites, and other dissidents were persecuted for their nonconformity. Most of them tried desperately to live lives of peace, but were persecuted unmercifully by the ruling Catholic powers. Though regarded as heretics, what filters through the main accounts—tendentious reports by their enemies—sounds suspiciously like sincere efforts at evangelical Christianity. They lived in constant peril from the persecuting state and the ecclesiastical structure of their time. They learned the meaning of Jesus words, " . . . when they persecute you in this city, flee ye into another" (Matt. 10:23). They were like the martyrs of Hebrews 11:36–38, and most of all, like their Savior. A few, as last resort, did resort to armed resistance.

As with many other aspects of Christian life and doctrine, our sources do not readily furnish us as much information as we might wish concerning the attitudes toward participation in military service of those Christians who were not a part of the Christian religious establishment during the Middle Ages. Revulsion against the senseless disorders and petty warfare of the times certainly brought many men of the upper classes into the various monastic systems.

The last of the large pre-Reformation separatist sects—the followers of John Hus (executed by burning in 1415), called Bohemian Brethren—began with nonresistance but ultimately took up armed resistance and thereby preserved a perilous existence and identity until the times of the Reformation.

CHAPTER 4
PEACE THOUGHT AND THE REFORMATION

The views of the main Christian groups at the time of the Reformation are relatively well known. The Roman Catholic, Lutheran, and Reformed views have been widely published. In recent decades the views of the Anabaptists—called the Left Wing of the Reformation (by Bainton) and the Radical Reformation (by George H. Williams)—have come to be better known.

It can now be said that opinion varied widely among all the Reformation peoples as to legitimate use of the sword. Opinions varied widely among the Anabaptists, from strict nonresistance to aggressive, militant, violent revolution.[1] It is doubtful that any new idea regarding war, peace, and nonresistance has arisen among Christians since Reformation times.

Legitimacy of police power, including the sword, by civil government was assumed almost universally. Medieval Catholicism had found both church authority and magistrates' authority in Jesus' words in Luke 22:38 regarding the two swords—one a secular sword (civil government), the other sacred (the church). Rational grounds were found in natural law and in the doctrine of creation. The medieval church believed it had a divine duty to declare truth to government. Government was not only to be guided by the church in matters of faith and morals; it was also to enforce church rules and edicts. There are even edicts from the papacy declaring that all civil rulers are under his authority as vicar of Christ.

Protestants found scripture guidance for a somewhat different doctrine of civil government and authority in Romans 13:1-7 and similar texts. They found practical and rational necessity for civil government in the biblical doctrine of sin: man is sinner and therefore violent and lawless; his violence and lawlessness must be restrained, and this is why civil government is necessary. Government, in late medieval thought, is necessary in order for man to be complete as man. He is complete only as *citizen.*

On the contrary, most Protestants believed government to be ordained of God to put a check on sin and thereby to make orderly society possible. Government is a result of the fall, not a feature of creation as originally constituted. I have dealt with these matters elsewhere.[2] Almost everyone during the Reformation age appears to have recognized the legitimacy of civil government with power of coercion and legitimate use of the sword—police, death penalty for certain crimes, war as last resort in national defense, and other just causes—in a world under the condition of sin. Most Christians today still recognize at least these limited government powers. The views of the first three centuries are hardly recognizable anywhere in the modern epoch, at least not within the major groups of Christians.

Within the general consensus, however, there were some differences among the leaders of the evangelical Reformation, even before the nonresistant wing of the Anabaptists entered the discussion with something of a consistent voice in the second generation, and quite apart from them. These differences, however, are not as great as sometimes made out to be.

Discerning men everywhere, including all the Reformation leaders, saw great evil in the warlike spirit of the times. Many humanist scholars, influenced not only by classical ideals (e.g., the Stoic doctrine of the harmony of the cosmos) and the Christian ideal of brotherhood under Christ and of common humanity as under God as Creator, wrote against the wars of the Reformation era. Without rejecting traditional just-war formulas, these men, most notably Erasmus of Amsterdam, hoped to reform Europe peacefully through education. Erasmus wrote a tract, reprinted frequently since, that makes a moving appeal for Christians to treat all fellow believers as brothers and to live at peace with them. Hence all wars should cease.

It is perhaps correct to say—as certain scholars do—that Luther was apolitical. He believed in coercive power of civil government as a divinely ordained means for maintenance of the temporal order, but not as a means to promote the church or the Christian life. Luther deplored the apparent necessity for protection of the Reformers by German princes. He was known to say to his best supporters among the princes that they needed his protection more than he needed theirs. He felt that public justice was imperfect because it was dealt by imperfect magistrates. But even though he deplored war, Luther came to support the emperor and the princes against the peasants in the early social wars. Luther's views partake of a paradoxical outlook which, without wishing simply to be pragmatic, are nevertheless practical. The ethic of suffering as ministry to man and of service to God is as plain in Luther's writings as in Thomas à Kempis' *Imitation of Christ* or in the latest writings of Christian pacifism.

Huldreich Zwingli, the Reformation leader of Zurich, Switzerland, contemporary of Luther, has been called *realpolitical.*[3] That does not seem quite fair, for it is not demonstrable that the moral relativism implied in *realpolitik* truly applies to this ethically sensitive man. H. J. Grimm correctly calls him Erastian.[4] "Zwingli believed in the use of political means for the attainment of Christian ends, but a theological pessimism [original sin] moderated his political enthusiasm."[5] Unlike Luther, Zwingli felt that it was not wrong to use civil power of the sword to achieve spiritual goals, even to promote ecclesiastical goals. Not surprisingly, the first Anabaptist martyrs received their crowns at Zurich. Reluctant to resort to war at first, in the last crisis of his career Zwingli accompanied Zurich's troops to battle and died on the field as a chaplain-combatant. He did so as chief pastor of the Grosmuenster Church of his city-state.

A generation later, John Calvin was very reluctant to approve of war as a means for Reformed evangelical Christians to compel Europe to tolerate the Reformed faith. This was true even when the Inquisition was making martyrs of Reformed Christians in France. Calvin taught the legitimacy of every form of civil government. Unlike some later Calvinists, however, he did not advocate violent overthrow of tyrants.

Calvin kept in close touch with the thousands of persecuted Reformed Christians (Hugenots) of France, suffering deeply under the kings of France and their papal advisors. Even in face of the martyrdom of hundreds, Calvin counseled submission, flight where possible, and nonresistant suffering. He taught his disciples to set their affection on heaven, not on the things of the earth. He provided no rational or doctrinal solution to the perennial problem of persecution by unjust government.

A considerable literature has recently emerged about Calvin, Calvinism, and the disorders of the time. He believed in the free sovereignty of the church under God. Though he also believed in the freedom of civil government from dictation by church or prelates, he insisted that magistrates should support and enforce public morality.[6] The Scots were his true sons when they confessed, "Mairover, to Kings, Princes, Rulers . . . wee affirme that . . . not only they are appointed for Civil policie, bot also for maintenance of the trew Religion, and for suppression of Idolatrie and Superstition whatsoever" (The Scotch Confession of Faith, A.D. 1560).[7] Wherever Calvinism in anything like its primitive form has penetrated, the leaders of society have sought actively to purify society in harmony with the ethics of Christianity. The power of the police and the court system has been employed more than once in this manner. It is no accident that a large number of Calvinist heroes are military men.

Anabaptist was the name given to a minority, but numerous, element in the Reformation who refused any alliance with the various territorial governments of Europe. They endorsed baptism of believers only (i.e., not infants) and the related principle that a local church is a body of believers gathered voluntarily out of a local community (i.e., not a territorial parish). The name *Anabaptist* was at first bestowed upon them by their enemies. They called themselves simply *Brethren*, sometimes *Baptists*. Before long, however, they accepted *Anabaptist* as a name for themselves.

Anabaptists of the first generation did not have a uniform doctrine of the sword—though certainly they were more nonresistant than militarist. Recent scholarship has convincingly shown that through the first generation after 1517, they had wide diversity in many doctrines. Being true Independents—without status—and mainly led by lay people, they were free to teach and live as they and their assemblies believed—provided they were willing to accept the consequences in an intolerant age. So several views of "the sword" flourished among first-generation Anabaptists. Some were willing to use the sword to establish the kingdom of God on earth. But most expected small support from civil government, for they shared Luther's skepticism about the righteousness of most princes and other magistrates. They were unwilling to follow the leading Reformers' endorsements of the coercive power of governments both to preserve public order and to prescribe the form of religion in their territories. Luther's prince gave him protective custody at a fortress called the Wartburg while he translated scripture. But there were no Anabaptist Wartburgs for a long time.

Much has been written in an attempt to sort out the many strands of the Anabaptist movement during the Reformation era. It now appears that the Anabaptists were interacting groups and sects, not a unified movement. This is acknowledged by scholars among Anabaptists, such as Walter Klaassen: "The main criticism of Mennonite classifications is that they are the result of efforts to push aside everything that does not agree with the somewhat arbitrary norm of 'evangelical Anabaptism.' One has the disturbing feeling that by 'evangelical Anabaptism' is meant Anabaptism as it ought to have been, seen through the spectacles of twentieth-century wishful thinking, rather than as it actually was."[8]

At any rate, the "pacifist" elements of Anabaptism were about all there was left after the shattering developments at Muenster in northwest Germany had come to a head. Radical Anabaptists took charge of government there. Their leading prophet predicted Christ's return in 1533 and the establishment of the New Jerusalem at Strasbourg. After a terrible siege, the bishop overlord captured the city (1535) and executed the leaders of the rebellion. Descendants of the continental Anabaptists who survived the persecutions are known as Mennonites, Amish, and Hutterites. They are numerous today only in the New World, mainly in the United States and Canada, with sizable groups in Mexico and Uruguay. All teach some form of the nonresistance doctrine and cultivate the practice among members. Dunkers (Brethren, Old German Baptist Brethren, and Church of the Brethren) arose out of pietistical movements in the Reformed part of Germany, coming to organized existence in 1708. They also migrated to America.

In their peace doctrine, all conformed fairly closely to the Swiss Brethren at Zurich. The leaders of the Swiss Brethren articulated their views in the early 1520s. Their best known statement is the Schleitheim Confession of 1527, which states that Christians must lay down "weapons of force, such as sword, armor and the like, together with all their use, whether for the protection of friends or against personal enemies." These Brethren did not deny the state the use of the sword but insisted that as true Christians they must not use it. They wanted to be obedient and cooperative, but not as part of the civil community. They were not only ethical and religious separatists; they wished to be social and political separatists also.

Present-day active involvement of these groups in specific social reforms, in spite of sympathy with anti-slavery, "temperance," and other movements, does not seem to be a genuine feature of their heritage from Reformation times.[9] It is a recent development. Historically they have been accused of lacking any social mission at all, though they deny this. Since World War II, especially in its aftermath, their "service committees" have done heroic and wonderful works of reconstruction.

In their social and political separation, the Swiss Brethren and Anabaptists differ from the Quakers. An offshoot of the seventeenth-century Puritan movement of England, the Quakers stood apart from the civil turmoil of the times. Like Erasmus of the preceding century, they believed that war is a resort to a sub-Christian ethics. Christians therefore should have nothing to do with it. Like Erasmus, but unlike the Anabaptists, they saw great hope for the future in having Christian rulers.

As for political activity, they would join gently in that fray to promote peace. Quaker William Penn and Pennsylvania (a Quaker State for several decades) are witness to their practical political activity. They also felt that by suffering as Christ did and for his sake, as well as by teaching, legislation, and public reform they could improve civil life and remove the causes of war.

The reforming temper of Quakerism was coupled with an optimistic view of human nature (the "inner light") as essentially peace-loving. Though they have not adopted the Anabaptists' separatist stance, the Quakers have employed many of the Anabaptists' and Brethren's arguments, thought to derive from Christ's example and teaching. Unfortunately, a large section of Quakerism became unitarian in theology long ago; more recently, others in the movement have shifted away from orthodox views. Hence, today much pacifist Quakerism appears to move in the same channels of thought and practice as liberal Christianity or even of secular pacifism.

Traditional arguments by these peoples are admirably simple. They appeal directly to what are deemed to be the plain words of scripture and the unmistakable example of Christ. This is no less true of their latest statements than of the confessions and publications issued during the sixteenth, seventeenth, eighteenth, and nineteenth centuries. For example, a Dunker General Conference (U.S.A.) of 1845 resolved that "in regard to our being altogether defenseless; not to withstand evil, but to 'overcome evil with good' (Rom. 12), the Brethren consider that the nearer we follow the bright example of the Lamb of God, who willingly suffered the cross, and prayed for his enemies . . . the more we shall fulfill our high calling and obtain grace to deny ourselves for Christ and his Gospel's sake, even to the loss of our property, our liberty and our lives." A Dunker tract published about 1900 presents "in support of the principles of non-resistance the following Scriptural facts: Christ is the 'Prince of Peace' (Isa. 9:6). His kingdom is 'not of this world' (John 18:36). His servants do not fight (John 18:36). 'The weapons of our warfare are not carnal' (2 Cor. 10:4). We are to 'love [our] enemies' (Matt. 5:44). We are to 'overcome evil with good' (Rom. 12:21). We are to 'pray for them which despitefully use [us], and persecute [us]' (Matt. 5:44)." The tract also cites Matthew 5:39; 26:52; Luke 9:55, 56. After quoting the familiar words of Paul in Romans 13 regarding the services of government and Christian duty to obey government, the tract adds the principle of separation to the principle of nonresistance, as follows: "The disciple of Christ . . . is subject *to* the higher powers, though he is not a subject *of* them. The kingdom of Christ is not of this world. The government is, or should be, in the hands of the moralist [not far from the Lutheran view that natural law and common sense should prevail in civil matters]. He stands between the righteous and the wicked, 'the minister of God to execute wrath upon him that doeth evil.' But when the moralist would join the kingdom of Christ, he must relinquish the sword."[10] The Christian is therefore not a citizen of his country *and* of heaven, but *only* of heaven.

This conviction has created the social isolation of peace churches of continental origin. It is the root of the earnest struggles of their posterity for some kind of integration with modern society—a society now hopelessly interdependent in many ways. In the past some of these sects have tended to form socially isolated groups, even to the extent of adopting the use of a special, plain costume for all members. If such groups remain small, the intellectual and social problems of political nonparticipation and social separation are manageable. When numerous enough to affect community political power centers, nonparticipation tends to drop off. If numerous enough to affect receipts at preferred or nonpreferred places of business, or if as business people themselves they seem to have competitive advantages, the principle of nonresistance is hard to maintain. Economic power bends only slightly to church discipline. It is simply unmanageable within their historic sect boundaries. It seems that nonresistance and separation, as understood by the Anabaptists of yesteryear, must always find its strength in weakness.

Because of their communal pattern, Mennonites in general and Hutterites in particular have been accused by neighbors of conducting unfair business competition, that is, economic war. They, on the contrary, have thought of themselves as merely going lawfully about their own business. Sensitive Mennonite pastors are to be heard instructing their congregations on Christian ethics in business and commerce. The living situation of these peoples may be observed in many prairie communities. Furthermore, these problems are being discussed in their own church literature, with considerable good effect.

CHAPTER 5
RECENT DEVELOPMENTS

Contemporary conservative evangelical representatives of the Mennonite and Brethren movements reject the political pacifism of our time.[1] In theory, at least, the "true believers" of these groups stand approximately where their ancestors did. They rejoice, as all Christians do, in every effort to create peace, but since they believe that man has a fallen nature, they have no perfectionist expectations.

Many official statements of the Brethren and Mennonites have allowed that God has given government the right and duty to use coercive force, even war, if necessary. They derive this teaching from the evident meaning of Romans 13:1–7. The Brethren were pioneers in colonial America. They printed selected *Minutes of Annual Councils* in 1876. From the 1785 annual council, the following minute appears: " . . . that the higher powers bear the sword of justice, punishing the evil and protecting the good, in this we acknowledge them from the heart as the ministers of God." It is hard to imagine a more resounding affirmation of the rightness of the power of the sword in secular civil hands. The same minute goes on to say, "But the sword belongeth to the kingdom of this world, and Christ says to his disciples, 'I have chosen you from the world. . . .' Thus we understand, with the beloved Peter, that we are to commit ourselves in all things that are not contrary to the will or command of God and no further."

It was the Baptists of British and American history who pioneered separation of church and state. Yet the continental Anabaptists were more radical than the Baptists. The Mennonites found early on that they could not maintain their distinctives and their existence in cooperation with the states of Europe. They sought only to be tolerated—allowed to live and preserve their mode of living—by the states of Europe. They continued in this manner until recently.

As pointed out earlier, social separation was affirmed by nonresistance doctrine in the peace churches migrating from post-Reformation continental Europe. They believed Christians are not of the world. The world is sinful. It is right for worldly government to wage war but sinful for Christians to participate in it. Old Testament Israel was a worldly commonwealth, or political entity, so its leaders and people were on many occasions commanded by God to wage war. But New Testament believers are never to think of their church as a political entity, never to promote it by physical force and, since the higher ethic of this spiritual kingdom must rule everything they do, Christians simply are never to fight in any physical way.

Christians in many denominations have believed the same way. Whether the position is logical or not seems unimportant to those committed to the teaching, as I have reason to know from personal experience. Can what is sin for a Christian be non-sin for a non-Christian? Most people, Christian and non-Christian, will have to say no.

Such rigorous separation has always been compromised to some degree, but the theory remains the same.

During the last two or three generations, nonresistance and separation practices have declined in America as in earlier generations they did elsewhere. The Unity of the Brethren (Hussite) laid aside these principles when nobility came into the movement.[2] Mennonites in the Netherlands became just another evangelical element in a homogeneous society—a deacon of the congregation at the Hague was the minister of the Dutch Navy and a Dunker, Martin G. Brumbaugh, was wartime (W.W. I) governor of Pennsylvania.[3]

The Brethren denomination which I know best is not atypical as far as conservative evangelicals of the peace churches are concerned. In the midst of World War II (1942), the National Fellowship of Brethren Churches—an energetically evangelical group of latter-day Dunkers—in an official statement acknowledged, "Some of our Brethren young men have already entered combatant military service. While this type of service is not in accord with the historic teaching of the Brethren Church, its acceptance is not made a test of membership nor a cause of discipline, because the church does not wish to coerce the consciences of men in such matters."[4] At about the same time, my professor of theology in a Brethren seminary taught us that Jesus' words about buying a sword authorize a limited degree of self-defense. Ministers in the denomination are sometimes former army and navy men, especially since World War II, and many of them serve in various branches of the military as chaplains.

By no means are all of the Mennonite and Brethren denominations still conservative evangelicals. The currents of thought and life affecting all Christians have affected them also, and not always more slowly. Theological liberalism (or what in America was called Modernism) began eroding commitment to the ancient faith in large sections of both denominations early in the twentieth century. This has brought about a changed view of both war and peace. Furthermore, the old nonresistance doctrine (coupled with social separation) now appears to find hard going against new activist forms of a socialist type of pacifism, and against the movement toward incorporation of these peoples into the political fabric of our times. We shall return to this theme.

CHAPTER 6
TOLSTOY AND THE NEW BREED

I attended college and university during the late years of the Depression, and first heard of Leo Tolstoy in a sociology class called "Social Reforms and Reformers." The professor at Washington Central College of Education in 1938 liked him almost as well as he did the Bolsheviks (communists), and that was with only slightly disguised admiration.

Leo Tolstoy (1828–1910), Russian novelist and social reformer, was born to a well-to-do family of Russian landed gentry. Though a university dropout, he was a gifted man and, while early engaging in some of the usual dissolute ways of the youth of his class, he lived a useful life. In his many roles—land owner, government officer, soldier, reformer, and religionist—Tolstoy was an example of unselfishness. He used his earnings as a novelist for what he thought to be service to his fellowmen. Tolstoy's books have been widely read, especially the almost interminable *War and Peace* and *Anna Karenina*.

A mover and shaker with the pen, Tolstoy's skill and fame as a writer have kept the public aware of him and hence given his ideas on religion and pacifism a kind of subliminal influence to the present day. He is of great interest to students of Christian nonresistance and active religious pacifism because he founded a form of liberal religion on what he deemed to be the genuine teaching of Christ.

In his autobiographical works Tolstoy reports that though he remained an Orthodox Christian, he became a skeptic at age sixteen. He always respected the moral teachings of the church, yet much in Russian Orthodoxy revolted him—the mixture of belief in God with superstition and sacraments particularly offended his intellect. The custom of bowing before images and relics disturbed him greatly. Tolstoy was very much repelled by his church's acceptance of war and capital punishment. After inwardly turning from his ancestral faith at age sixteen, he never fully returned to belief in any supernatural religion.

But Tolstoy was a genuinely religious man. His religious views were pervasive, if only implicit, in his great works of fiction. In autobiographical works he explicitly propounded his new, private faith and spread it worldwide to readers and admirers.

The religious doctrines of Tolstoy's scheme of things started with the premise that Christ's disciples, being unlettered men, inaccurately recorded their master's teachings long after his death. So "it may be assumed that the church in accepting the three synoptic gospels had accepted much that was inaccurate."[1] Even after the disciples wrote them, the Gospels went through many changes, he said. Therefore he argued that he could justly eliminate the Gospels' sectarian elements, elements introduced to support what the churches already believed and such like—all foreign to the teachings of the real Jesus. Tolstoy was sure he could eliminate anything that offended "common sense" or that seemed to him morally unacceptable or superstitious. By this process of literary reduction he isolated the core of genuine Christianity. To Tolstoy the substance of Christianity is " . . . the inculcation of love, humility, self-denial and the duty of returning good for evil. . . . The Sermon on the Mount as reported in Saint Matthew contains . . . the essence of Christ's teaching which Christians should carry out entirely. The key to the sermon is . . . 'Resist not evil.'"[2]

Tolstoy rejected all miraculous elements in the Gospel accounts and reduced Christ's teachings to five "entirely new" commandments: (1) "Live at peace with all men"; (2) "Thou shalt not be united physically to any woman except the one whom thou hast originally known sexually"; (3) "Swear not at all" (which he took to be rejection of binding power of courts, as well as oaths of soldiers, public officials, and the like); (4) "Resist not evil"; and (5) "Love your enemies."[3]

C. T. H. Wright summarizes on Tolstoy's fourth and fifth points: "Christ's followers were never meant to act as judges, citizens, policemen or in any other capacity in which it would be their duty to resist evil. Christians should do good in the sense of living virtuously. . . . they should never return violence by violence."[4]

Tolstoy taught that what is usually thought noble and great—patriotism, defense of one's fatherland—is really despicable and an infraction of the law of Christ. He regarded the doctrines of original sin, atonement, the Trinity, and the resurrection as without historical or rational foundation and contrary to true Christian teaching.

It is impossible fully to summarize the views of a man who wrote more in his lifetime than many people read in a lifetime. The sort of consistent pacifism that Tolstoy promoted, however, is plain: the force a policeman employs to restrain the violent is as wicked as the rapist's or robber's—presumably also the force a parent uses to restrain a rebellious child. According to Tolstoy, all physical force is wrong.

There are many affinities between Tolstoy's views and the liberal forms of Christianity which developed in Germany during the long life of Tolstoy and which later were imported to Britain and America. One of the period's most outstanding and influential liberals, Adolf Harnack, published his lectures on *The Essence of Christianity*—the ripe fruit of decades of study and writing—about a decade before Tolstoy died. Harnack's summary of the essence of Christianity employs a reductionism similar to Tolstoy's and comes to similar results as regards Jesus and the religion he founded. If Tolstoy had been a German, he might have qualified as a somewhat errant disciple of Harnack—much of their general outlook is similar, though Harnack does not endorse pacifism of the Tolstoy type.

Tolstoy has been succeeded by a new breed of contemporary pacifists, somewhat backslidden from orthodox Christianity, who are much like Tolstoy in their pacifist teachings.

These writers operate chiefly within the historic peace churches but outside the authentic succession of separatist nonresistance. Their ancestors were genuine biblicists; whatever else these authors and teachers are, they are not biblicists. Their brand of "peace" scholarship is at open war with conservative scholarship; it has grown up in full harmony with radical methods of New Testament criticism. There is affinity of thought with the social analysis and economic theories of Karl Marx (anticapitalism, socialism) and the positivist programs of Auguste Comte, as these movements have developed in secular academic and political circles.

The most widely read Christian pacifist today is John Howard Yoder of Goshen Biblical Seminary (Mennonite). Yoder has made some startling declarations. Instead of concurring with the near universal denial that Jesus announced a political program, Yoder strenuously affirms that he did. He says that the announcement of Jesus at Nazareth, near the beginning of ministry, that he had come "to preach the gospel to the poor . . . to preach the acceptable year of the Lord" (Luke 4:18, 19) was to proclaim that the Year of Jubilee, when all Jewish people were released from debt and other encumbering social obligations, was now to be extended to all Christians. According to Yoder, the program is not found in "remodeling the total society; . . . [it is in] the political novelty which God brings into the world . . . a community of those who serve instead of ruling, who suffer instead of inflicting suffering. . . . This new Christian community in which the walls are broken down not by human idealism or democratic legalism but by the work of Christ, is not only a vehicle of the gospel or fruit of the gospel; it is the good news. It is not merely the agent of mission or the constituency of a mission agency. This is the mission."[5] A high claim, indeed!

In a widely read book, the same author tries to root his programmatic interpretation of Jesus' mission in the law of Jubilee. If I read him correctly, Yoder would have us lay aside our "time-bound" understanding of justification. Justification is not, says he, a divine act whereby a sinner is forgiven; it is not forensic, but practical. He asserts that John Wesley and Sören Kierkegaard, along with many existentialists and conservative evangelicals, might simplemindedly follow Luther's "mistake" of thinking about justification in terms of "personal rightousness," but such are preoccupied by personal concerns. Now, however, "biblical scholarship of this century . . . found more freedom to distinguish between the initial cultural context of a biblical passage . . . and the contribution it makes to contemporary thought. . . . If we may be freed by self-critical scholarly objectivity no longer to assume that the authority of the Bible resides in its saying things we agree with [and John Howard Yoder knows that he is thus freed!], we may be free as well to hear more clearly what it really says instead of giving it credit for saying what we already think."[6] If we are thus free as are Yoder and his acknowledged exegetical advisors (Krister Stendahl, Markus Barth, H. W. Bartsch, and Paul Minear), we would see that Galatians and Romans teach a justification that is, as such, a breaking down of barriers between men. Justification is a "social phenomenon."[7] Hence the peace doctrine of this particular pacifist has apparently become his gospel. This is truly closer to Tolstoy than to the Bible. (See Appendix on page 58.)

This line of thinking is attractive by reason of daring and novelty, though it has little to do with gospel consistency or biblical simplicity. It is not surprising to find this author's name associated occasionally with several avant-garde, left-leaning "evangelicals." But those Swiss Brethren of Schleitheim and Zurich would hardly recognize the company. What must orthodox Mennonites think?

Yet it must be said that J. H. Yoder writes a persuasive page if his rhetoric is given a chance to catch the reader up and carry him along. One famous evangelical, U.S. Senator Mark O. Hatfield, has taken Yoder's argument from the Year of Jubilee quite seriously, though without coming to all of Yoder's conclusions.[8]

Jacob J. Enz is a similar pacifist Bible interpreter, apparently a Mennonite. He thinks that "if pacifism is not found in the very fabric of biblical thought, no amount of proof-texting will be convincing."[9] Employing some of the same techniques as Yoder does and with much acknowledged help from the "Acts of God" theology of G. Ernest Wright, Enz thinks he so finds such pacifism.

I am impressed by the zeal and obvious sincerity of these writers, but not with their evidence for the sort of pacifism they believe in. It is not the same faith their ancestors had.

A pacifist disciple of Yoder and apparently former student is Ronald J. Sider. His chief interest is in a program of what he believes is Christian aid to all earth's poor. He would establish a program like Karl Marx's "from each according to his ability to each according to this need." Sider devotes six pages of his *Rich Christians in an Age of Hunger* to answer the question, "Is God a Marxist?"[10] He quotes several texts of scripture as well as a contemporary evangelical theologian writing in the pages of *Sojourners* (Feb. 1976, p. 31) apparently to show that God does endorse Marxist views of economics.[11]

But Sider's earlier passion was pacifism of the type advocated by Yoder. It is set forth vigorously in Sider's *Christ and Violence* (Herald Press, 1979): government is not an ordinance of God woven by him into the structure of the world in order to restrain sin, as Protestant theology has always held, but is rooted in the "principalities and powers" that are a part of the created world order. Hence government must be "subject to the risen Lord Jesus" and establish justice in the world. For Sider this means an essentially Marxist-Socialist world order.[12]

The scheme of how this is to happen including the end of war by nonmilitary national forces of some sort, is not fully worked out. But near the close of the book Sider unveils his own vision of how it should be worked out among the historic peace churches. He observes that their separatist-nonresistance stance is now inadequate and apparently out of date. He declares that "the Historic Peace Churches lack an adequate theology of power."[13] After setting forth what he thinks is an adequate theology of power he then proposes that churches and Christians "take the offensive" through political action (lobbying, voting), economic strategy (boycott), and civil disobedience to compel (coerce) our governments to abolish war and establish peace and justice. As for all Marxist thought, to Professor Sider justice means equality.

(It is no mere happenstance that not only in Asia, Europe, and Africa but also in North and South America the economic leveling of people at a much greater level than mere subsistence has accompanied Reformation Christianity. These great political and economic benefits have grown chiefly where the gospel and the Bible went first and were given opportunity to blossom.)

In 1982, several years after *Christ and Violence,* Ronald Sider and Richard Taylor collaborated to publish another book (*Nuclear Holocaust and Christian Hope,* Downers Grove, Ill.: InterVarsity, 1982) to furnish further explanation of pacifism and a program for putting pacifism into effect among national governments. This book, advertised as "a book for Christian peacemakers," carries the pacifist program far beyond the church. About seventy pages of it are devoted to concrete proposals as to how a national government can and should defend its people against aggressor nations without military force. It is to be wholly nonmilitary, yet employing active—not passive—resistance. The authors prefer an expression used widely in other pacifist literature of our time: *civilian-based defense* (CBD).

In *Nuclear Holocaust* Sider and Taylor propose no policy of nonresistance to evil such as one finds in the historic peace churches and even in the Bible. The authors' ideas are merely a sophisticated brand of secular pacifism with a religious twist. Their goal is admittedly noble and would be great if someone could make it work. The Bible, however, nowhere instructs the powers that be—whether Christian or otherwise—to lay aside what Paul called the "sword" and to exchange it for CBD.

Nuclear Holocaust closes with four chapters on nonmilitary defense by CBD, plus twenty-three pages of fine-print guidance into the literature of pacifism, names of pacifist organizations, and educational materials. The authors seem to have not omitted anything.

More recently Sider's fertile mind has found tentative ways to unite the war-peace issue with the abortion issue. Perhaps soon he will find several other logical riders to his pacifism bill.

Sider quite unexceptionally sees that some nations are poor while others are prosperous. His proofs are, of course, impressive. Where he and his fellow socialists fail is in providing a proper background in history for the disparity and a convincing analysis of the cause. It will not do simply (if lavishly) to call the facts about world hunger to our attention, then propose a solution through simple transfer of income.

A full discussion of a Christian view of economics is beyond the scope of this study. Economics has something to do with war, of course, but it is not the "be all" of Marxist and socialist theory. Let us try to put this in perspective.

It is a matter of common knowledge that the nations which have escaped mass poverty are almost all of the "Christian" West; that they did this within the last two hundred years; that the Protestant lands—especially Britain and the former British parts of North America—led the way; and that these lands have what has been called democratic economies. In this regard, the contrast between Anglo-America and Latin America is inescapable.

Michael Novak, a contemporary Roman Catholic lay theologian, has done more than any author I know (not excluding scholars such as Ernst Troeltsch and Max Weber) to spell out the details of these differences and to explain them. Volumes now pour forth from his citadel in the American Enterprise Institute. In his recent *The Spirit of Democratic Capitalism,*[14] Novak shows that the democratic economies of North America and Europe have escaped poverty not through special material resources nor by conscienceless exploitation of undeveloped countries and the like. He shows that their relative affluence came through a marvelously beneficial combination of three factors: (1) an honestly democratic variety of political systems, mothered in Britain and extended elsewhere; (2) a biblical, Christian moral and ethical understanding of life as a whole; and (3) an economic base in free competition–private enterprise. These three factors condition one another and produce an expanding material economy.

Ideas like these are not new. Earnest Reformed writers have expressed themselves similarly. Even Vermont Royster, whose columns have appeared in the *Wall Street Journal* for decades, lifts his pen to write like this. I wish his column of early June 1983 might be read by all who think El Salvador's civil war or Honduras' poverty can be cured by simple sharing of funds, technology, or anything less than a new spiritual culture.

The writings of J. H. Yoder and Ronald Sider and of many other "new breed" religious pacifists have strong affinities of thought and temper with the theological and political liberalism one encounters in the forty-year-old liberal journal, *Christianity and Crisis.* (This was not the case when Reinhold Niebuhr, a truly profound theological thinker, used to publish his thoughts contrary to liberal pacifism in early issues of the journal.) The very daring of their arguments (if not their biblical consistency) gives them great appeal today among a large number of persons raised in a shallow biblicism and educated without theological depth. The authors seem sincere and they speak and write with apparent conviction. They seem to bring respectable scholarship to their writings.

We can learn from them. We should be impressed by their zeal and apparent sincerity, but not by the kind of pacifism they teach. It is not the faith of their orthodox ancestors. And their following is small among those close to their historical Pietist and Anabaptist origins in doctrine and practice.

Pronouncements of the World Council of Churches (WCC) have followed near to what I have called the "new-breed" line. WCC agencies were especially active in making antiwar pronouncements during the Vietnam War.

The Fourth Assembly of the WCC (July 1968) officially adopted a principle of selective conscientious objection. The idea is that any one who objects to a particular conflict should have the right to refrain from participation in it on grounds of conscience. United States selective service regulations allow exemption only on the grounds of conscientious religious objections to all war. They do not allow one to pick his "bad war" and be excused from military service in it.

Nearly every denomination and other religious group in America endorses the notion that citizens should be excused from military service if conscientiously opposed on religious grounds. The WCC statement, however, unlike most church statements, shifted the ground of objection from biblical and religious convictions to "the full application of religious liberty to individuals and organizations and the free right of expression of conscience for all persons, independent of creed or belief." This is said to be "important for all human freedoms."[15] The 1983 Pastoral Letter of the Roman Catholic Bishops of America also endorses the idea of selective conscientious objection, though with some reserve. The Lutheran Church-Missouri Synod adopted a resolution in 1969 to provide protection for "conscientious objectors to specific wars" (See W. A. Nix, "The Evangelical and War," *Journal of the Evangelical Theological Society*, Summer 1970, 135).

Harold E. LeVander, then governor of Minnesota, was a delegate to the Fourth Assembly, sent by the Lutheran Church of America. He opposed the Council action, saying, "I think selective conscientious objection is a very dangerous innovation. The conscience is quite an elastic thing, and we may find ourselves endorsing people who feel they should stay out of a war because they have a family or think that they have an important job."[16]

William F. Buckley, Jr., reacted to the WCC move in an article in the *New York Post* (July 20, 1968). With his usual skill, Buckley pointed out that putting "the sanction of Protestant Christianity behind the movement to permit individuals to select the wars they desire to participate in [has the practical effect of encourging] defiance of the laws of the United States." He went on to say that in addition to encouraging civil disobedience, it creates a moral problem, having "the effect of saying that wars are justified if they are wars of personal passion." He argued that this undermines respect for authority, for "the individual becomes not merely the absolute moral arbiter on whether he is (as a pacifist) prepared to commit violence under this particular circumstance." If the individual does not agree with duly constituted authorities, he would have the right to excuse himself. Buckley points out that such a stance appears to eliminate the role of the state in deciding when force is necessary, actually encouraging a kind of anarchy or even vigilantism: "If a Christian is going to deny the role of the impartial mechanism of the state in making binding decisions involving the use of violence—whether war, electrocution, or tear gas—then what is to prevent the individual from asserting his own conscience at such moments when the conscience declares that he believes violence to be necessary?"[17]

Buckley's last point, similar to Governor LeVander's objection, is correct, as subsequent WCC actions amply prove. WCC funds and agents have been supporting lawless guerrillas at several spots around the world. Also, in view of the reported Jesuit support of revolution in Latin America, one can understand why in 1968 the Rev. Donald R. Campion, editor of the Jesuit weekly *America*, endorsed the WCC action.

Swift changes and reactions have followed the WCC actions of 1968. Even some conservative evangelicals are beginning to write and talk about a theology of resistance to oppressive government.

How do contemporary representatives of the biblical faith of the historic Anabaptists and Dunkers (Brethren) feel about all this? They most heartily reject the distinctive features of all forms of Tolstoyism and what Norman F. Gordon has called "A New Breed of Conscientious Objectors." They feel that the new Brethren and Mennonite "pacifists" have betrayed their churches, even if a majority should follow after them. Gordon has called their teachings "Satan's counterfeit for the doctrine of nonresistance." He affirms, "True Christians have never advocated the doctrines of present-day pacifism. The pacifist aims to establish a better world by eliminating war; he attempts to bring peace and harmony among the unregenerate nations of earth . . . through political influence. . . . He believes in the innate goodness of man."[18] The same author goes on to reaffirm the traditional "ancient" faith of the Brethren and Mennonites that the sword, including the right and duty of waging war on necessary occasions, has been given to governments by God. The unregenerate masses must be held in control by the sword since they reject God's Word, he says.

Gordon closes his remarks on "new breed" objection to war by saying: "It is clear . . . that the older concept of the principle of conscientious objection was based on the individual's responsibility to God and the principles set forth by Him in scripture. The position taken by the World Council of Churches is based upon purely human considerations and takes the theological position of the innate goodness of man—a doctrine totally rejected by the Word of God."[19]

APPENDIX
The Pacifism of *The Politics of Jesus*, by J. H. Yoder

Ten years after its publication, John Howard Yoder's *The Politics of Jesus* (Grand Rapids: Eerdmans, 1973) is still an important book. Some disciples of Yoder among leaders of the new "peace movements" seem to have the serene confidence that the pacifism of this book is eternal truth, the essential gospel of the kingdom of God announced by Jesus in the Gospels. This truth was written in scripture but nearly sealed from common understanding until Yoder published it in 1973. His views seem now to reign among liberal Mennonites, and he has recently addressed "peace-movement" gatherings in Germany, along with Jim Wallis the leftist editor of *Sojourners* magazine. I judge this book to be the most important of Yoder's several books and the most significant pacifist publication of our time.

Yoder shows considerable rhetorical skill as he assembles his case. His book contains as wide a selection of the writings of contemporary liberal New Testament scholarship as one is ever to read in a single book intended for popular consumption. Avoiding as much scholarly jargon as he can, he skillfully weaves it all together. At the very end of the book he states what he thinks he has proved:

> *A social style characterized by the creation of a new community [church] and the rejection of violence of any kind [by anybody at all] is the theme of New Testament proclamation from beginning to end, from right to left. The cross of Christ is the model of Christian social efficacy, the power of God for those who believe. (p. 250)*

There is, of course, much that is simply Christian in that summary and some that is standard Christian pietism of Anabaptist flavor. But there is also what appears to be an only partially developed new religion whose gospel is a novel form of pacifism based upon a special sort of liberal critical reinterpretation of the New Testament. Yoder employs polemical skill in stating his case in such a way that a Christian can hardly reject the statements. Yet if the author's implications were carried out, it would amount to a whole change of religion, if one's religion is any historic form of orthodox Christianity.

I shall attempt an evaluation of *The Politics of Jesus*—not a complete summary of Yoder's argument, which is somewhat technical and involves synthesis of many advanced liberal New Testament critical studies. Often he plainly asserts that his reinterpretation rests wholly upon the insights provided by "scientific" or "modern" critical techniques. He pays his debts throughout the book to specific critical writers, many of whom reject any truly miraculous revelational content in the Bible.

I submit a few assertions to illustrate and provide evidence for this evaluation of Yoder's book:

1. For Yoder, the Christian collective society is the only important reality of the Christian religion. Justification, for example, is simply something one has only in concert with other believers. It also involves the breaking of barriers between races and peoples, indistinguishable from reconciliation between believers.

2. Atonement, for another example, is something *demonstrated* by Jesus' crucifixion, not an act that righted a wrong relation between an offended God and sinners. Jesus' death was a demonstration of how not to use political power to secure one's own advantage over other people. It has nothing to do with objective guilt or forgiveness of an individual man's sins.

3. The New Testament was misinterpreted for centuries as having to do with the sins and personal salvation of individuals. This is false; the problems the Bible really treats are collective structures of power and how believers can corporately overcome them. The *Christus Victor* theme (i.e., Christ triumphant over principalities and powers) is a major theme of the New Testament. These earthly principalities and powers are the sinful but created powers (i.e., all "establishments") that on earth rule over men. All use of power (violence) to coerce behavior is wrong.

Such startling specific claims and negations are sometimes followed by concessions that there might *also* be something valid in the older orthodox ways of interpreting this or that aspect of doctrine. For the author, however, the older has no apparent value:

1. He brushes aside all the older assessments of Jesus' ministry and would compel his reader to adopt the new approach by belittling anything else:

> *Jesus was not just a moralist . . . ; not primarily a teacher of spirituality [rejects older liberalism]; he was not just a sacrificial lamb preparing for immolation, or a God-Man whose divine status calls us to disregard his humanity [first he caricatures, then he rejects orthodox doctrines of the work and person of Christ]. Jesus was in his divinely mandated (i.e., promised, anointed, messianic) prophethood, priesthood, and kingship the bearer of a new possibility of human, social, and therefore political relationships [this means Jesus' primary mission was directed toward new here-and-now human, social, and political changes]. Men may choose to consider that kingdom as not real, or not relevant, or not possible, or not inviting; but no longer [i.e., since Yoder has put together for us the transcultural meaning of the Gospels] may we come to this choice in the name of systematic theology or honest [Yoder is honest!] hermeneutics. (pp. 61, 62)*

2. The gospel proclaimed by Jesus was a program to abolish debts, liberate imprisoned debtors, and redistribute capital. The "forgive us our debts as we forgive our debtors" prayer is literally a financial statement. Yoder teaches literal redistribution of capital accumulations:

> *Evidently Jesus accepted voluntary poverty for the sake of the kingdom and ordered his disciples [it must be all right for the human Jesus to order people around, even if no one else should] to practice the jubilary redistribution of their capital [cites Luke 12:30–33]. No one doubts that he said this. All that is debated is whether this redistribution of capital was commanded by Jesus for all Christians in all times and in all places. (pp. 74, 75)*

Yoder *knows*—what indeed he must, if his doctrine is not to make nonsense—that this particular "order" of Jesus

> *was to be put in practice here and now, once, in A.D. 26, as a "refreshment," prefiguring the "reestablishment of all things." (p. 76)*

Obviously such a procedure adopted generally and evenly would put an end to all commerce, ownership of goods and property, and the like, without which organized civilization could not go on.

3. Yoder's treatment of nonviolence in view of the Old Testament wars is basically quite similar to standard pacifist treatment found in Mennonite theology, *but with a difference.* He says,

> *Whether the taking of human life is morally permissable under all circumstances was not a culturally conceivable question in the age of Abraham or that of Joshua. (p. 80)*

His outlook on the literature, history, and theology of the Old Testament seems to be about the same as found in Gerhard Von Rad's *Old Testament Theology* (Edinburgh, London: Oliver and Boyd, 1962, pp. 79, 80).

4. On the necessity of Jesus' crucifixion:

> *His vocabulary and picture of what must come to pass were much more "political" than they were "existential" or cultic [i.e., related to the political, economic, and class struggles of Palestine 1,950 years ago]. His disavowal of Peter's well-intentioned effort to defend him cannot be taken out of the realm of ethics by the explanation that he had to get himself immolated in order to satisfy the requirements of some metaphysically motivated doctrine of the atonement [as in Reformation creeds and evangelical doctrine]; it was because God's will for man in this world is that he should renounce legitimate defence. . . . God's Man in this world was facing, and rejecting, the claim that*

the exercise of social responsibility through the use of self-evidently necessary means is a moral duty. (p. 100)

Thus Yoder sets aside orthodox understanding and places his pacifist doctrine at the center of the gospel. As he says elsewhere in the book, nonresistance is the gospel.

5. In view of these statements from the first one hundred pages—there are many similar ones throughout—his disclaimers of any charge of rejection of orthodox doctrine seem ineffectual. Before quoting one of his several defensive disclaimers, I draw attention to one more flagrantly sarcastic treatment of any orthodox doctrine of atonement: for him an orthodox understanding of the death of Jesus as propitiation of the divine wrath or atonement is "some kind of cosmic hocus-pocus." This man's mastery of sarcastic invective is almost without parallel in recent scholarly writing.

At the climax of a defense of his own *Christus Victor* interpretation of Jesus' death, he makes strong claims for his own new approach to Colossians 1:15–17:

With this observation we have found one more point at which the ethical relevance of the stance of Jesus breaks through in a segment of the apostolic literature for which generations of most Protestants did not know how to deal. The Powers (political, economic, etc., on earth among men) have been defeated not by some kind of cosmic hocus-pocus but by the concreteness of the cross; the impact of the cross upon them (politicians, wealthy people, all wielders of human power) is not the working of magical words (such as "this is my body," at the communion table) nor the fulfillment of a legal contract calling for the shedding of innocent blood (a caricature of vicarious atonement), but the sovereign presence . . . of Jesus. (p. 162)

He goes on to say that the church is a structure and a power, and should act in society as Jesus did (a rather peculiar form of the "moral influence theory" of the meaning of Calvary). This is the gospel according to Yoder.

On page 232 and elsewhere Yoder asserts that his words about a gospel without atonement, a justification that is social and not forensic, a reconciliation with God apart from any necessity for shedding innocent blood, and faith as obedience, not an act of heart commitment, are not to reject "traditional" doctrines, only to correct past one-sided emphases. The claim sounds hollow. His voice is the voice of liberalism. Yoder's peace doctrine reads like the theology of a new religion, something *different from* rather than *supplementary to* historic Christianity.

PART TWO
A New Agenda

CHAPTER 7
MAKING UP OUR MINDS

Early in this book we surveyed the nonresistance-to-evil stance of the first century Christians and summarized the reasons why they took their costly stand. With due respect we shall now evaluate their arguments and assess their actions in the context of their times and ours, their understanding of scripture and ours today.

Were their reasons for nonresistance adequate? Was their interpretation of scripture correct? Granting that their work of faith and labor of love is praiseworthy, is it incumbent on believers of every age and nation to do the same? Is their religious (not political) pacifism to be received as a doctrine? May it be a special "vocation"—in the Reformers' sense of the word—or perhaps only a useful strategy for the believer under oppressive pagan government?

As we noted earlier, the views of prominent Christian leaders of those early centuries on some other questions are outrightly rejected by most believers today: the developing emphasis on salvation by moral life and rule-keeping (*legalism*), dependence on rites called sacraments for salvation (*sacerdotalism*), and transfer of all liturgical acts and church government to a priestly class (*prelacy*). Few of us would accept Tertullian's rather exotic eschatology or Cyprian's incipient papalism. Why then accept their nonresistance doctrine? The fact that they were saintly people does not render their beliefs and practices a model for constructing Christian doctrines. While everyone is interested in respectful inquiry into the beliefs and practices of the Christians of the generations immediately following the apostles, no scholar today takes their opinions on doctrine and interpretation of scripture as necessarily correct.

Almost immediately after the Christians of the Roman Empire received legal status, the leading churchmen began to give the magistrates advice on how to conduct themselves in office. They wrote letters to them about how to behave as Christians in civil leadership. They told them to straighten out their sexual and marital relationships, to tell the truth, and to rule with justice.

The church fathers also spoke and wrote to civil rulers regarding resort to military force in governing their Empire. The Empire was then so large that except for warding off some invading "barbarians" (our ancestors, in the main) the most severe military engagements had been in what Augustine called social wars and civil wars. In the century before Jesus there had been a frightful civil-social war (the deciding battle near Philippi) that led ultimately to Julius Caesar's triumph and the passing of Republic into Empire (Octavius-Augustus), which prevailed when Jesus lived. Even in Jesus' time war had become mainly a policing action, meant to keep the peace in the Empire.

Against such a background, Ambrose of Milan, followed by Augustine of Hippo formulated a doctrine for the use of coercive force by magistrates. It is a distinct mistake to suppose that Augustine did his research, then struck out and wrote a monograph on the "just-war" idea in the manner of a Reinhold Niebuhr or Paul Ramsey. Contrary to what some scholars claim, Augustine did not synthesize ancient philosophy and biblical doctrine into a just-war theory. In fact, one must read twenty or more of his letters and tracts (plus innumerable comments on biblical texts) to understand fully his views. They come nearest to synthesis in scattered portions of *The City of God,* especially Book XIX. In his introduction to *The Political Writings of Augustine* (Chicago: H. Regnery Co., 1965), Henry Paolucci rightly emphasizes the practical rather than theoretical character in Augustine's writing: "Technically precise descriptions of governmental institutions and . . . constitutional forms are conspicuously absent."

Though his advice to the Roman citizen or magistrate drew from the accumulated secular wisdom of his own time and place, Augustine intended above all to be scriptural. It is another mistake to suppose that what among theologians is called "just-war theory" has some plainly traditional connection with Augustine, simply because he was the first to spell it out somewhat plainly.

Many sincere men of several epochs have personally enacted the same transition that believers of Augustine's era underwent. Born in milieus of what is called "nonresistance"—social and political separation—history simply forced them to think through and act out a transition from it. As far as I can discern, many peace church youth of my generation—the one which was born during World War I and which fought World War II or supported it on the home front—did just that.

I had just entered seminary when the headline **WAR IS ON** in the newspaper *Extra* shocked us on that September 1, 1939. I spent the next six years as a student in seminary and as a pastor. On V-E (Victory in Europe) Day I was already a seminary professor. I preached the community V-E Day sermon. I also had read **WALL STREET CRASH** on the headline of my father's copy of the newspaper in October 1929. So I have vivid recollection of ten years of worldwide economic depression and six years of worldwide war. Our decisions in those days affected more than economic advancement or job satisfaction. Survival was the issue.

By 1941, when the draft began, I was forming my own opinions about the peace doctrine. By 1946, or shortly thereafter, my doctrine took the approximate form it still has. Then, as now, I came to differ from several inherited opinions that I still nevertheless respect. When what we believe affects how other men perceive us to be (bold, brave, cowardly, foolish, wise, consistent, inconsistent, orthodox, heterodox), caution and soft-speaking become the order of the day, and I wish to follow that order. When among the sturdy, sincere, good people of the historic peace churches, as I frequently am, respect for their history of courage and devotion, frequently leading to martyrdom, rises in my heart. Somehow I then have small inclination to persuade them out of their beliefs. Their characteristic social isolation (now dissolving) could never be universal for Christians anyway. Many of them are persuading themselves out of it. Yet seen from the inside it seems quite admirable.

In the following pages of this book we shall be considering the facts and arguments that all Christians must consider in making up their minds about what is right for them to do by way of support or nonsupport of the coercive power of government.

CHAPTER 8
WARS OF THE OLD TESTAMENT

The Old Testament presents difficulties to those who argue for nonresistance and pacifism.

The ideal of civil order and prosperity among the nations, of every man dwelling quietly with his neighbor without violence, did not wait for the New Testament to be announced in scripture. As the peace church writers remind us, peace is the fruit of obedience in Old Testament stories and teachings. The great poetic passages such as Isaiah chapters 2 and 35 bring the peace ideal into sharp focus. They show that nonviolence is the consistent Old Testament ethical standard for holy people.

Having said this, however, we must also acknowledge that some of the saints frequently engaged in physical conflict and that wars were a part of the necessary work of noble, morally sensitive kings. But even admitting this, many peace church spokesmen contend that the Old Testament does not lend any support to the notion that war could ever be right for any Christian, in or out of public office; it is always sinful for a Christian to take up arms either in self-defense or in defense of country. How then do people who accept the Old and New Testaments as equally God's Word dispose of the apparent discrepancy? Following is a summary of the peace churches' chief arguments in this regard.

Among authentic Anabaptist and Brethren groups, these arguments are ordinarily supported by straightforward acceptance of the truthfulness of the Bible—it contains no subtleties of interpretation. Their writers insist, as do the Reformers and most orthodox Protestants, that the scriptures are essentially perspicuous to anyone who intelligently and carefully reads them. One needs the teachers of the church, to be sure, but one should be suspicious of any "guidance" that requires the lay believers to explore complicated, arcane theories of origin and authorship. One should not concern himself with what "J" or "P" or the "primary Redactor" or "Deuteronomist" or "Chronicler" or "priestly historian" had in mind when one reads a scripture passage. These orthodox writers employ four main scripture arguments:

1. The first argument is one commonly met: *God has a right as judge and ruler of the world to command his people to shed blood in war. These occasions, however, set no acceptable precedent for any Christian to take human life apart from such a command.*

A Quaker booklet published circa 1950 affirms "that God, in His own right, did delegate men to take life seems certain. In such case God was using men instead of storm or flood or earthquake to bring about His judgment on the wicked. The only justifiable wars are those undertaken in obedience to the plain, clearly-expressed command of God."[1] This author and the many preachers who have affirmed the same are certainly correct if Jesus and the New Testament truly condemn all participation in war. The same would be true if biblical inferences require that Christians always refuse to use physical force. In following chapters we shall consider whether such is the case.

2. A second argument, a kind of hypothetical assertion, is succinctly stated by Guy Franklin Herschberger: "*What God prescribed in one dispensation God could forbid in another.*" *Granting that Old Testament people of God may have been commanded by God to take up weapons of war, in the present age God's people are strictly forbidden to do so.*

Sometimes this view is not stated quite so starkly; rather, it is supported with overtones of "progress of doctrine in the Bible" or "progressive revelation." It is difficult to find serious objections to this argument. In an article appearing in the *Mennonite Quarterly Review,* Waldemar Janzen acknowledges that "the Old Testament expects wars to take place. Israel's participation in war is taken for granted on the whole." Scriptural representations of God as "Man of War" or "God of Armies" are mainly "language about God . . . borrowed from human language." Yet of some wars "the Old Testament clearly states that God himself commanded them" (1 Sam. 15:1–3 is cited). Thus God "waged [these wars] himself, using Israel as his sword."

"Great acts of God though they be when seen as means to bring to pass the divine purposes, they are emergency measures when viewed within the economy of sin and salvation." These wars anticipate the final manifestation of the kingdom of God, when he will put down every contrary principality and power. "The Old Testament sees war as an expected part of human existence and as such accepts it, albeit not unquestioned, for its own time." Yet the believer today is on different ground: "He still lives in a world of warfare, the warfare which is to culminate in a great final conflict between God and the powers of evil. . . . The Christian, as the Israelite of old, believes that God fights his wars and enlists his people in them. The weapons of his warfare, however, are now not swords or guns, for the warfare is directed against the principalities and powers, a warfare the weapons of which are spiritual" (quotations above taken from "War in the Old Testament," by Waldemar Janzen, *Mennonite Quarterly Review,* vol. 46, 1972).

Another stout defender of nonresistance is Herman A. Hoyt. A past president of a Brethren seminary, Hoyt insists that Jesus did indeed change the law, " . . . in this case, Christ Himself . . . with sovereign authority changes the law for His church. 'Ye have heard that it was said, An eye for an eye and a tooth for a tooth. . . . But I say unto you, Resist not him that is evil.' . . . He was the One who gave the Old Testament Law, and He has the right to change it."[2] He goes on to say Christ not only changed the law, he raised it and enlarged it.

This interpretation neglects the plain fact that the Mosaic requirement of an eye for an eye and a tooth for a tooth was a rule for magistrates to use in enforcing penalties for the breaking of public law. It never was designed as a ground for private vengeance. This author believes firmly that public officials should use the Mosaic principle of "the punishment must fit the crime" as a righteous requirement of public law in all dispensations.

Hoyt acknowledges that the "problem is very real, and it is useless to set it aside without some good reason."[3] He proceeds to supply not one but three reasons. First, "Israel was a nation of this world while the church is a spiritual nation not of this world." It was right, he claims, for the worldly nation Israel to do what "the church"—which "is not such a nation"—must never do, that is, to use physical force to defend itself.[4] The author seems to forget, however, that even the most military-minded theologians hardly suggest that the church take up arms. The question is whether individual Christians should do so in the service, not of church but of country.

Like a good son of pietist tradition, Hoyt emphasizes that the Christian homeland is heaven and that heaven and its King "need no material or human protection."[5] Apparently he does not know that Calvin and Luther made similar assertions but did not thereby claim exemption of Christians from public duties, including military service. Most people who think this way certainly believe that churches need protection against thieves, vandals, and corrupters of public morals, which police and national armies help to provide. Even Mennonite, Quaker, and Brethren churches need such protection and do not usually deny it. If it is right to pay taxes to *pay* police and soldiers (as Paul seems to say in Rom. 13:1–7), why is it not equally right to *be* policemen and soldiers?

Hoyt supplies another reason why he thinks the law of the Old Testament was really changed by Jesus. He claims that New Testament believers, being regenerated, are indwelt by the Holy Spirit—as the Old Testament believers were not—and are therefore given the means to attain a higher standard (nonresistance) of conduct.[6] But did Jesus and the New Testament forbid the bearing of arms by Christians on every occasion, whereas the Old Testament believers were not so forbidden? True, a higher standard of conduct might seem appropriate for a time of better spiritual resources, but that is no concern to the central issue: Is the New Testament standard a different one from the Old Testament standard?

A third argument seems only to restate the first except that the differences between Israel and the church are phrased specifically in terms of alleged differences between "the dispensations of law" and "the dispensation of grace." Hoyt again assumes that Jesus' words ("Resist not him that is evil") proclaim a change of divine law. It is plain, however, that Moses' principle for administration of justice in public law is as valid today as it ever was. Most scholars believe Jesus was simply correcting erroneous and perverted use of the Mosaic provision in a time of deep spiritual apostasy.

3. *The many wars of Israel in the Old Testament were not the will of God but were made necessary by Israel's disobedience to the will of God.* This argument, employed by many generations of Mennonites and Quakers, holds that God promised that if the Israelites would obey him, "I will drive out" the inhabitants of Canaan (Exod. 34:11). "Behold, I send an angel before you, to guard you and to bring you to the place which I have prepared" (23:20, RSV); "When my angel goes before you, and brings you in to the Amorites . . ." (23:23, RSV). Moses declared, "The Lord your God will send hornets among them, until those who are left and hide themselves from you are destroyed" (Deut. 7:20, RSV) and further, "You shall not be in dread of them; for the Lord your God is in the midst of you, a great and terrible God" (7:21, RSV). Thus all the wars of conquest in the last months of Moses' life—as well as under Joshua and later leaders—were wars in disobedience to God's will or at least rendered necessary by chronic disobedience. Before World War II a fine preacher named Theodore Epp—for many years heard around the world—set this argument forth vigorously in a booklet published by a Mennonite press.[7]

We must agree it is undoubtedly true that Israel's chronic disobedience, plus the perversity of its rulers, were the causes of much of the warfare. Yet it is hard to read the Book of Joshua without gaining the distinct impression that what Joshua and the chieftains of Israel did in annihilating the Canaanites was exactly what God had intended all along and commanded them to carry out.

Whatever may be made of selected cases, two of their wars—both under the leadership of Moses—were expressly stated in the scripture to have been at God's command, wholly at the Lord's initiative. The first was during the first weeks of the wilderness travels; the second during the last weeks. These bloody episodes are exceedingly drastic in their divinely commanded execution. To say that all of Israel's wars were caused by disobedience is clearly impossible, in the light of this evidence. It is significant that pacifist-nonresistance treatments of this argument frequently omit all reference to these two episodes—the Amalekite war (Exod. 17:8–16) and the war of extermination against the Midianites (Num. 31:1–54). These two wars simply will not adjust to a pacifist scheme of the world or to reductionism in biblical hermeneutics. I quote briefly from the biblical account of the Midianite episode, which is the most impressive in this regard: "The Lord said to Moses, 'Avenge the people of Israel on the Midianites; afterward you shall be gathered to your people.' And Moses said to the people, 'Arm men from among you [a thousand from each tribe] for the war, that they may go against Midian, to execute the Lord's vengeance on Midian'" (Num. 31:1–3, RSV).

Throughout Numbers 31 every warlike initiative can be traced to God. It can only be said that Israel was avenged (v. 2) and God was avenged (v. 3) by the annihilation of every member of the tribe of Midian. It was the sparing of lives of "all the young girls who have not known man by lying with him" (v. 18) that came from human initiative, God condescending to the Israelites' desires in the case. No wonder this chapter is skipped in the usual pacifist treatment of scripture.

4. The principle of progressive revelation is called upon to assist the peace church treatments of the Old Testament. On this basis they explain that *while war may have been at least excusable of old, such a low standard has been superseded by a much higher level of revelation in the New Testament.* Paul Mills, cited earlier, states this frequently affirmed teaching clearly enough: "These men did not have as great an opportunity to know the full will of God as we have since the giving of the New Testament. Abraham was a polygamist and a slaveholder; so was David. Yet will any Christian argue that

because these Old Testament saints practiced polygamy, concubinage, divorce or slavery that it was the will of God for them? And because God winked at certain ignorance or overlooked it will anyone dare to contend that a Christian may practice the above vices with impunity? Why then, will we plead so for war when it is just as plainly stated to be displeasing to God?"[8]

There is certainly a progress of revelation in the Bible and it is true that in many ways the New Testament sets forth a more spiritual standard of behavior than the Old Testament allowed. This, however, is of doubtful relevance to the issue at hand unless there is a changed status of civil government as well. But civil government is as much the bearer of the sword as ever in God's order of preservation in a fallen sinful world. The real question does not concern a higher moral standard for godly people, but the relation of God's people to civil government. The question is one of fact within the New Testament itself: Does the New Testament specifically forbid Christians to participate in personal self-defense and in civil military action?

We have already observed that a "new breed" of activist, militant, religious pacifists has arisen in the denominations representing the "left wing" of the Reformation. These leaders are more than a little contemptuous of the simple biblical faith and orthodox doctrines of their ancestors of the Mennonite churches. John Howard Yoder, whom we have met earlier in these pages, is exceedingly sarcastic and biting in criticism of any approach to scripture and doctrine which he feels is less than critical and modern. Yoder apparently feels that Calvin, Luther, and other old-timers are perhaps excusable for their shabby orthodoxy, but no Christians living today have this same excuse, especially with the guidance provided by recent biblical criticism and the doctrinal guidance of his own preferred type of liberated theology.

Another of the professors at the Associated Mennonite Biblical Seminaries of Elkhart, Indiana, is Dr. Millard C. Lind. Lind has produced a sober, methodical study of the "pacifism" of the Old Testament in the form of a biblical theology of warfare in ancient Israel, entitled *Yahweh Is a Warrior.*[9] It is in the style of the "biblical theology movement" popular in the 1950s and 1960s and which was promoted in the journal *Interpretation.* The literature Lind cites is especially respectful of the "Baltimore School" of William Albright, G. E. Wright, John Bright, D. N. Freedman, and the scholars whom they have taught, as well as the usual cluster of American and European writers whose works are stock in trade of the movement. Not so radical as the older literary criticism of the Wellhausians and quite different from "uncritical" liberalism, there is a sincere effort on the part of these scholars at an historical understanding of the Old Testament. They seek to combine the essentials of the document-development hypothesis with the ongoing fruits of archaeology and historical studies.

In the introduction to Lind's book J. H. Yoder observes that "any point" the book makes must be with "historically aware interpreters. . . . For this reason Lind takes account of documentary hypotheses and the various historical reconstructions . . . since the age of Wellhausen. There are other precritical or noncritical reconstruction ways of reading the Old Testament—Jewish, Catholic, and conservative Protestant ways—but by the nature of the issue, his choice in favor of the encounter with critical alternatives on their own terms, was the only right one."[10]

Yoder's remarks truly set the stage for Lind. Although the author follows a somewhat chronological treatment, the analysis is not of literary portions in order, but essentially of layers. These layers are the supposed documents of the Wellhausian analysis as modified and updated. Lind is not interested in what Moses had to say but asks questions such as, What did the J compiler or the Deuteronomist or the priestly historian have in mind when he included such and such an incident or gave such and such an interpretation of an event?

Nevertheless, most of Lind's results are not objectionable. The Old Testament is indeed fundamentally *pacific.* Lind uses the word pacifist, but he demonstrates only that the Bible promotes peace more than war: that its leading lights—from Abraham, Isaac, and Jacob on to Jeremiah—avoided wars. He makes good on his contention that sometimes the "holy wars" of the Old Testament were cases where God *alone* fought. The people might have armed for battle, but only God acted—the crossing of the Red Sea, for example.

When the forces of Sisera (Judg. 4) were defeated by the stars in their courses—a natural flooding of the battlefield is the usual interpretation (5:4, 20, 21)—it was without the force of Israel's arms. Lind reminds the reader that Jael, who killed Sisera as he slept, was probably not an Israelite. So he makes a pretty good case for some military victories of Israel's God quite apart from employment of human weapons in Israel.

But this new kind of pacifism, in my judgment, fails at the same points that the older and orthodox nonresistance interpreters do—by giving too little attention to the passages that fall outside their understanding of how things ought to be. However pacific Abraham may have been, he was not a pacifist, for he organized a small army of his retainers and, by a swift military expedition, rescued his nephew Lot, along with his family and neighbors (see Gen. 14). Lind plays down the incident, even though there is a whole chapter of Genesis devoted to it. He suggests it may "have entered the tradition in the time of David" to tie the city of Jerusalem to the patriarch "as well as give precedent to David's wars."[11] Similarly, Lind seems embarrassed by Moses' acceptance of a military role for Joshua in the war with Amalek (see Exod. 17).[12]

In Numbers 31 we see an even more explicit example: God specifically commands Israel to carry out a bloody war of extermination against the Midianites. The background for the Midianite War appears in Numbers 25. Here we discover that it was a war to help ensure the family integrity of the Israelites against fornication and idolatry. This is so important to the nation destined to produce the mother of our Lord that an irresistible temptation to fornication was removed by extermination. Phinehas' execution of a fornicating pair—an Israelite male and Midianite female—was praised by a Mosaic oracle from God (Num. 25:6–18) and celebrated in Psalm 106:30, 31.

Moses directed the war and 120,000 Israelites carried it out with the divine blessing. Lind passes by this story completely. Yet he treats the Songs of Miriam and Moses (Exod. 15) and of Deborah (Judg. 5) at great length. The main reason he assigns for this emphasis is that these two poems are held to be contemporary with the events described in these books, yet are much more ancient than the narratives in which they are imbedded (according to the critics followed by Lind). Numbers 31, however, is not honored even by a sentence. One cannot but suppose that this passage simply does not fit Lind's views about the way the story ought to be. If this is not the case, then why is this outstanding narrative of one of Israel's wars skipped over?[13]

There is a positive gain from Lind's careful research. He makes it plain that there is no basis in scripture, even on the principles of the modern critical views of the origin of scripture and the history of Israel, for assuming that Israel had the same violent tradition of "trust in chariots" and of religious subservience to a state policy of military aggression that prevailed among the great nations of antiquity. Even the great Gerhard von Rad cannot make it so.[14]

In the judgment of most reverent students of the Bible, the Old Testament advocates the protection and tender support of human life. Death was not in the scheme for man in the original created order of things. It is a ghastly intrusion, as abhorrent to God as to man, but necessary to the divine holiness and to the ultimate good of the created order of things. Death, however, is a penalty required by God's holiness (Heb. 9:27). Death of mankind—whether brought about by natural causes or by other men—is the wages of sin (Rom. 6:23).

God is against violence resulting in the death of mankind. One of the reasons for the coming of the Flood was that "the earth was filled with violence" (Gen. 6:11). After the Flood a first order of business was the divine establishment of government of man by man with death penalty for the crime of murder (9:16). This was apparently not only an external law proclaimed by God, but also something planted in man's psyche, like the command to be fruitful and multiply, so that some form of social organization (not necessarily a state in the purely modern sense) with coercive restraints on violence on the local scale would follow wherever mankind would go. (In the Mosaic scheme for Israel in Canaan, civil government was almost wholly a village and tribal affair. Monarchy was established because of Israel's backsliding.)

"The dreadful consequences of failure properly to punish all deliberate murderers according the Mosaic Law's requirements are constantly reiterated. Several chapters in the Pentateuch are devoted to careful instruction in the handling of murder cases (see esp. Exod. 21:12–25; Lev. 24:17–21; Num. 35:9–34; Deut. 21:1–9). In this connection it is important to understand that murder is held to pollute the very land whereon the people dwell, as does fornication; further that the only way to rid the land of the pollution of first degree murder was by the death of the murderer, officially inflicted by civil action after due process of law. 'So shall ye not defile the land wherein ye are: for blood it defileth the land: and the land cannot be cleansed of the blood of him that shed it. Defile not therefore the land which ye shall inhabit' (Num. 35:33, 34; cf. Deut. 9:15; 19:10–13; 21:1–9). . . . the prophets of both the kingdom of Israel and the kingdom of Judah pronounced coming judgment because of murder unpunished by the responsible magistrates of both kingdoms (cf., e.g., Jer. 2:34–37; Hos. 1:4; 4:1–5)."[15]

The pacifist and nonresitance writers are certainly correct in contending that Israel's history, including its many wars, is marred continuously by disobedience; hence war was used as judgment on Israel—when defeated—and many successful wars of defense and of conquest would not have been necessary. These teachings, however, are common to all orthodox interpretation of the Old Testament, as far as I can determine. Those who contend that Israel's "holy wars" were of the same type and on the same moral-political-religious plane as the wars of the god-king rulers of Assyria, Egypt, and other ancient Near Eastern nations are not orthodox Protestants but the more advanced liberal-critical interpreters. An example is Gerhard von Rad's two-volume *Old Testament Theology* of 1962. In this work he tests the historicity of events in Bible history by "the omnicompetence of Analogy" and thinks such testing to be the chief task of biblical criticism. The much more conservative Martin Noth, though he employs the "orthodox" documentary analysis, usually accepts the testimony of the "sources" (*Exodus, A Commentary*, Philadelphia, Westminster, 1962). By the rule of analogy with ancient Near Eastern neighbors, von Rad determines "that to understand the rise of Israel the critic must assume that the 'real history' of Israel's beginnings was more or less the same as that of other nations, and that in the case of the [Red Sea] event Israel fought hard just like other people had done." In von Rad's view, any uniqueness of Israel's religion was not caused by the juncture of word and deed in actual historical event, but by a later theological reflection that reconstructed past history. Von Rad held that the Red Sea episode was reconstructed by J (the so-called Jehovist writer of one of the basic documents of the Pentateuch) as a result of the fundamental changes that took place in Israel at the time of kingship, especially the development of the Solomonic "enlightenment," which reflected the influence of international wisdom literature on the Israelite religion.[16]

All of this discussion about documents and critical history will have value only for the few who are versed in such technical matters. In plain words, what does it mean?

It means that according to Exodus and on through the Old Testament, the Lord alone is King of Israel. The nation was formed by the exodus from Egypt and accompanying events. The first "war" of the nation showed that God was king and sufficient protector and deliverer. Israel was without the usual weapons of war, as far as we know, and was pressed into a hopeless situation—the sea before them, Pharaoh's chariotry pursuing and closing in on them. In this dreadful crisis God delivered the people *monergistically* (working alone), not by means of human armies. "Moses said unto the people, Fear ye not, stand still, and see the salvation of the Lord, which he will shew to you to day" (Exod. 14:13). The song of victory (Exod. 15) assigned the victory to God and to him alone, no human hand having been moved to save them.

If von Rad is correct, these events never happened. During Solomon's reign, a time of relative international peace, there was an increase of borrowed knowledge in Israel. Thus the pacific idea of victory without human warfare was borrowed from Israel's pagan neighbors![17]

God did not mean for Israel's history to be as bloody as it was: this is not a strange notion to any person who takes the

Old Testament at face value. Yet, as we have already shown, there is clear teaching that the theocratic nation was to exercise coercive police actions as all other nations; that it was to execute deliberate murderers, in harmony with divine law for all the nations; and that on occasion it was to engage in war. The biblical record, for example, clearly states that the tribes of Israel were directed to drive out the Canaanites. On occasion, God directly commanded them to wage war. The later books of the Pentateuch provide detailed rules for waging war. In Deuteronomy 20, for example, we see that under Israel's lawful rulers war was a just action, to be waged and participated in with all good conscience. It is also evident that such wars were not always a monergism—God acting solely—without human soldiers and weapons:

> *When thou goest out to battle against thine enemies, and seest horses, and chariots, and a people more than thou, be not afraid of them: for the Lord thy God is with thee, which brought thee up out of the land of Egypt. And it shall be, when ye are come nigh unto the battle, that the priest shall approach and speak unto the people, and shall say unto them, Hear, O Israel, ye approach this day unto battle against your enemies: let not your hearts faint, fear not, and do not tremble, neither be ye terrified because of them; for the Lord your God is he that goeth with you, to fight for you against your enemies, to save you. (Deut. 20:1–4)*

Comment is hardly necessary. The chapter goes on to describe recruitment of soldiers, verbal negotiations with the enemy, what to do if the enemy city capitulates, siege, and treatment of the populations of conquered cities. It closes with some rules for siegemaking.

Contrary to common opinion, Old Testament believers lived under an ethical system in which any act of personal revenge was proscribed. Under the settled conditions of the wilderness encampments or residence in Canaan, self-defense was permitted, with severe limitations. Brotherly kindness to one's neighbors—both compatriots and foreigners—was encouraged by Mosaic religion. What the priest and

Levite did in Jesus' Good Samaritan parable was contrary to the spirit and letter of Mosaism. Passages such as Romans 12:19-21 exude the very atmosphere of peace; but in this they are similar to Mosaic religion as I have sought to show elsewhere.[18] Hermann L. Strack and Paul Billerbeck, in their unique *Kommentar zum Neuen Testament aus Talmud und Midrash* (Munich: C. H. Bechsche Verlagsbuchhandlung, 1959) provide seven pages of parallels to Romans 12:14-21 from Old Testament and rabbinic sources (pp. 297-303). A large part of the passage is quoted directly from the Old Testament. For example, Proverbs 25:21, 22 is quoted: "But if thine enemy be hungry, give him bread to eat; if he be thirsty, give him water to drink: For thou shalt heap coals of fire upon his head." The great King David was rebuked for even contemplating revenge on Nabal. The great Joab was executed by Solomon for an act of revenge; he shed the blood of war in time of peace. After Moses, the Jewish "citizen" had access to public law for justice; if that failed, he still did not have the right to take matters violently into his own hands, though self-defense from attack was not denied him. But use of physical force was limited, even in defense of property—a proprietor could not slay a daylight burglar obviously bent on theft only. A nighttime burglar, whose intentions were not obvious, might be slain.

Now comes the question: In the Old Testament dispensation, if the ethic which allowed limited personal self-defense, vigorous action against insurrection (e.g., Absalom) and just wars was not inconsistent with a personal ethic of nonretaliation and nonviolence to the neighbor; may not the same be true in the New Testament dispensation? The answer seems to be yes. Most Christians have always thought so. I grant that many who are convinced of traditional nonresistance will remain unconvinced by these evidences. Yet it seems just to ask them to regard with a kindly eye the beliefs of the much larger number of believers. They ought at least to consider the evidence without prejudgment.

CHAPTER 9
THE PRINCE OF PEACE

The sayings of Jesus about such matters as revenge, self-defense, response to threats of violence, and the like have always been near the center of the biblical pacifists' arguments. Further, no conscientious Christian can come to terms with his own conscience without making some decision as to what these sayings mean, their personal relevance, and what to do about them. These passages are the ones employed by "peace church" preachers and authors to demand their idea of the nonresistance of all of Christ's disciples. They seem to place the issue clearly on the level of discipleship, or, put another way, on the level of the lordship of Christ. The issues are often put to members of Mennonite and Brethren congregations in exactly these terms.

"Biblical pacifism results from Christian discipleship. Refusal to fight is based on my calling as Christ's disciple. Jesus is Lord. . . . Christ demonstrated the way of peace in contrast to war and retaliation. . . . The Sermon on the Mount is the essence of Jesus' teaching and it is picked up phrase by phrase throughout the New Testament, calling for obedience here and now."[1] These words are by John Drescher, of Eastern Mennonite College (Harrisonburg, Virginia).

There is an unbroken line of faithful devotion to this approach; it can be traced back to the very Anabaptist martyrs at Zurich in the 1520s. The same direct, literal simplicity endorsed and practiced by these peoples has produced other almost equally widespread and nearly uniform beliefs. Following are a few such beliefs: refusal to take any oath, in court or otherwise ("Swear not at all," Matt. 5:34); washing of feet in connection with the Lord's Supper ("I have given you an example, that ye should do as I have done to you," John 13:15); the holy kiss as a custom ("Greet one another with a holy kiss," Rom. 16:16, RSV); refusal to hold public office (" . . . they are not of the world," John 17:14); and nonrecourse to law and civil courts ("And if any man will sue thee at the law, and take away thy coat, let him have thy cloak also," Matt. 5:40).

As we have seen, a high degree of general social isolation was a normal feature of many "peace churches" for several generations. Those who followed the Anabaptist way found it necessary to support one another closely, while they asked the rest of the world only for tolerance and such economic liaison as was necessary to commerce and exchange of goods. They participated very little in common community life. This was the uniform shape of Brethren (Dunkers) and Mennonite history until recently. These forms of the faith still flourish in many Mennonite and Hutterite communities where the old teachings persevere nearly unchanged, at least as far as outsiders can see.

We shall not consider all the sayings of Jesus. Our attention may rightly be focused on Matthew 5:33–42; out of this passage, so heavily worked by biblical pacifists, we shall concentrate on verses 38 and 39: "Ye have heard that it hath been said, An eye for an eye, and a tooth for a tooth: but I say unto you, That ye resist not evil: but whosoever shall smite thee on thy right cheek, turn to him the other also." These words bring the matter of nonresistance to focus.

Jesus did not originate the biblical advice against excessive litigation, casual use of oaths, contentiousness, and personal vengeance. Such advice is in the Old Testament as early as the Pentateuch. But Jesus undeniably put these Mosaic ideals into a more purely spiritual perspective (as opposed to purely pragmatic). Moses made several statements about nonviolence in personal disputes, but he also established a coercive civil structure for handling such problems. (One is reminded of the English Pilgrims of Plymouth Colony and their Mayflower Compact of 1620 for the civil government of their colony.) Yet he discouraged excesses in litigation. Jesus' statement in Matthew 5:38, 39, when considered in its proper context, is quite similar to what Moses advocated. Jesus was not writing new rules. When he referred to the Old Testament saying "An eye for an eye, and a tooth for a tooth," he was calling attention to the fact that such a philosophy should not be misused for personal vengeance. Let us look more carefully.

The Old Testament saying cited by our Lord is part of a larger Pentateuchal precept that appears several times in the legal section of the Hebrew Bible. The first occurrence (Exod. 21:24, 25) is in a clear context of guidance to civil magistrates on the execution of public law. In the specific case, civil judges are being guided in assessing penalties when a fight has occurred between two men with resultant harm to themselves or to others. A glance at the larger context by the reluctant assessor of my arguments will assure him or her that the text is being correctly represented. The key portion reads, " . . . he [the culprit] shall be surely punished . . . and he shall pay *as the judges determine.* And if any mischief follow, then thou shalt give life for life, eye for eye, tooth for tooth, hand for hand, foot for foot, burning for burning, wound for wound, stripe for stripe" (21:22–25, italics added).

This text has nothing to do with personal revenge. The statute was to guide civil judges in courts of public law, not to license private people for private adjustment of grievances. It was meant specifically to prevent personal revenge. The principle set forth is that in public law, penalties exacted should be in proportion to gravity of offenses committed.

In Leviticus 24:20, where the law appears again in condensed form, again the subject is penalties for breaking public laws. Examples are furnished, with the welcome provision that penalties should be the same for both natives and foreigners (24:22). The passage closes with a drastic historical case—divinely authorized execution by stoning of a man convicted of deliberate blasphemy (24:23). The third (and last) occurrence of this law (Deut. 19:21) is even more specific than the former two: the context supplies witnesses, litigants, judges with priests present, official inquiries, testimonies, and assessments of penalties (19:15-20).

According to Mosaic law, in cases of capital punishment for certain crimes, the execution was carried out by the whole congregation—the Lord's people in the community where the crime was committed. If the crime was blasphemy, child sacrifice, apostasy, incorrigible rebellion against parents, certain types of violation of marriage, and flagrant Sabbath-breaking, the whole community was to assemble and execute the criminal by stoning him. People designated as "witnesses" were required to cast the first stones. The community of faith was not at all distinct from the political commonwealth. Thus the disagreeable duty involving coercive, death-dealing force could not be assigned to someone else. Conscientious objection let no one off the hook. (See also Deut. 7:5-7; 22:21; Lev. 20:2-21; 24:16; Num. 15:32-36.)

Thus in Matthew 5:38, 39 Jesus may have been rebuking the way people then stood scripture on its head to get support for their vengeful impulses. In doing so he emphasized a feature of public law under which Jews of the time were ruled. Consider, for example, the trials and execution of Jesus himself, as well as the stoning of Stephen.

This Mosaic teaching is praised in the Proverbs: "Say not thou, I will recompense evil; but wait on the Lord, and he shall save thee" (Prov. 20:22), and "If thine enemy be hungry, give him bread to eat; and if he be thirsty, give him water to drink: for thou shalt heap coals of fire upon his head, and the Lord shall reward thee" (25:21, 22). This Old Testament passage is quoted by Paul in Romans 12. Paul thereby adopts it as his own doctrine. Yet this New Testament truth is no "higher" than that of the Old Testament.

God-fearing Israelites were aware of a clear distinction between *personal* behavior—which was to be noncoercive and without recourse to physical force, except under very unusual circumstances—and the duty of their *public officials* to apprehend and punish lawbreakers. In addition to the Mosaic rules and Proverbial advice against taking vengeance, the Israelites had some outstanding public examples among their best leaders. Whose temper does not rise with David's when he fiercely exclaimed of the churlish Nabal, "He hath requited me evil for good. So and more also do God unto the enemies of David, if I leave of all that pertain to him by the morning light any [male]" (1 Sam. 25:21, 22)? Yet the wise and comely Abigail, though she acknowledged that in semi-civil capacity David sometimes fought the Lord's battles, reminded him that he was without authority to wreak *private* revenge. David relented and responded, "Blessed be thy advice, . . . which hast kept me this day from coming to shed blood and from avenging myself" (25:33). Shortly afterward "the Lord smote Nabal, so that he died" (25:38). Later, as a civil magistrate, David many times carried out severe penalties (even execution) on lawbreakers in good conscience and with divine approving sanction.

These facts of history and of revelation must be brought to the Sermon on the Mount. All Jesus' hearers were familiar with the strict limitation on use of force for private persons *qua* private persons. These same private persons when serving in a public, civil capacity as officers and magistrates were commanded to use such force as was appropriate and necessary. In Matthew 5 Jesus is clearly speaking of the former (private action of believers) not the latter public capacity. All the weight of previous biblical revelation supports this distinction. Therefore Jesus' remarks under consideration here are irrelevant to the question of participation in war.

Is everything to be interpreted flat-out literally? Consider this saying of Jesus: "If any man . . . hate not his own father, and mother, and wife, and children, and brethren, and sisters, yea, and his own life also, he cannot be my disciple" (Luke 14:26). No one takes these words as literally intended.

Granting that teachings in Matthew 5:38, 39 refer to personal conduct, not to enforcement of public law, there is another large area to consider: the question of interpretation. What did Jesus mean by the vigorous, sensuous, image-bearing language of the Sermon on the Mount? "If thy right eye offend thee, pluck it out, and cast it from thee. . . . And if thy right hand offend thee, cut it off. . . . Whosoever shall smite thee on thy right cheek, turn to him the other also." It is in the context of this turn-the-other-cheek saying that the following critical phrase appears: "But I say unto you, that ye resist not evil" (Matt. 5:39).

Is every one of these vivid sayings to be interpreted literally—sober-faced, word-for-word? It is safe to say that no competent teacher or writer of any school thinks so. No competent interpreter I know of holds that Jesus meant literally, under any circumstances, for anyone to gouge out his own eye or to cut off his own hand.

Nearly all commentators agree that Jesus was lifting the level of conduct for God-fearing people from mere legalistic conformity to heart-felt, deeply motivated fulfillment of God's will. (Paul reiterates this principle in Romans 13:9, concluding with an Old Testament saying: "Thou shalt love thy neighbour as thyself." A verse later he adds, " . . . therefore love is the fulfilling of the law.") Jesus was calling his listeners back to the true spirit of their own law, correcting the legalism to which every moralistic, separatist group is liable.

In interpreting such passages, commentators generally call attention to the Hebrew culture of the audience and Jesus' Hebraic manner of speaking, observing that strong figures of speech are characteristic of such discourse. Special attention should be given to *hyperbole* (transparent exaggeration for effect). Jesus used hyperbole often, and everybody understood that he did. How else could one understand hating one's parents, giving all your clothing, following departing guests for long distances, lending everything covetous neighbors ask for? These words were never intended to be applied literally.

What Jesus says in Matthew 5, however dear to Christians, and however distinct and unique in certain respects, is not entirely new. It is quite similar to many precepts and examples of the Old Testament and ancient Jewish literature wanting in this regard. Strack and Billerbeck provide nearly three pages of citations and documentation of parallels to one saying: "Agree with thine adversary quickly" (Matt. 5:25) and so on throughout the whole Sermon on the Mount. Jewish scholars rightly protest that Jesus never spoke more fully in ancient rabbinic fashion. And some of them would even like to claim Jesus as a first-rate rabbi and reduce him simply to that.

Also, as seen earlier, "biblical pacifists" like to find their particular doctrine in the Old Testament. It is true that the Old Testament contains much *pacific* teaching, as well as praise and predictions of peace between men and nations. But these pacifists ought also to acknowledge the presence of divine authorization and approval of at least some wars, as well as the participation of saintly men in wars and in capital punishment of criminals.

In this regard Ronald Sider, a contemporary "new breed" pacifist who also tries to be biblical, has made many concessions. He is not in every sense a "defenseless" pacifist, as is demonstrated in the latter pages of his *Christ and Violence.* Perhaps he will move further toward a genuinely whole-Bible point of view.

Jesus himself did not behave as a literal interpretation of his sayings would require. For example, when smitten on the cheek, he did not invite another blow but responded in protest, "If I have spoken evil, bear witness of the evil: but if well, why smitest thou me?" (John 18:23). If we look only at the words, Jesus did not obey his own precept, for he did not turn the other cheek. Yet he had come to Jerusalem prepared not only to be smitten but to be crucified by men, for whose forgiveness he would pray to God (I am paraphrasing Augustine here). Jesus also spoke in his own defense here. Furthermore, although in the Sermon on the Mount he said, "Swear not at all," he accepted abjuration, being put under oath at his own trial (Matt. 26:63).

Even Paul seems to have failed to obey the Lord's command, for when struck on the face during interrogation he cried out to the high priest, "God shall smite thee, thou whited wall: for sittest thou to judge me after the law, and commandest me to be smitten contrary to the law?" (Acts 23:3). This was hardly turning the other cheek.

I think most people who reflect on all these evidences will be convinced, as I am, that such precepts of Jesus should be related to the heart and feelings, rather than to external procedures. We must always act in the spirit of Christian meekness, grace, and kindness: "As much as lieth in you, live peaceably with all men" (Rom. 12:18). This means we should have regard for the true good of people rather than simply to give them what they say they need or to yield to their every demand. Blind submission was not what Jesus had in mind when he said, "Resist not evil" (or, "Resist not the evil man").

As a child I often accompanied my father as he met disoriented Indians who would drive their buggies, followed by their dogs, onto our rented Yakima Indian Reservation ranch. Never in his life did my father turn away a hungry Indian, but he never granted their demands for cows, horses, seed grain, and the like—the very sources of his economic power to pay the rent. To his ability he met the true needs of those unhappy people and honored the true intent of his Lord's instructions quite exactly. In turn, the Indian landlord thoroughly respected him. My father certainly had penetrated the meaning of Matthew 5:42: "Give to him that asketh thee, and from him that would borrow of thee turn not thou away."

From our brief inquiry, two conclusions follow: (1) Early Anabaptists and many modern pacifists interpret Jesus' precepts as requiring of Christians rigorous nonresistance to evil; their interpretation, however, is faulty. Also extrabiblical is the doctrine of rigorous nonparticipation in civil life and functions—that is, social separation. In his Sermon on the Mount, Jesus did not absolutely forbid use of physical force to legitimate civil government, and did not forbid believers to serve in their countries' armies when called upon to do so. The new breed of politicized, peace-church activists senses this, even though one suspects that the precise meaning of Matthew 5 is not very important to them. They believe in resisting what they deem to be evil with every tool at their disposal, short of outright physical violence. They caricature their opponents, and there is no scarcity of invective and censorious treatment of all those whom they deem opposed to their system of thought. (2) The Mosaic ethic for private persons severely restricted recourse to physical force but required participation in public executions of criminals and sometimes in war. In Israel there was a personal ethic as well as an ethic for civil government. They existed side by side without conflict and contradiction among God's people then.

There seems to be no conflict or contradiction in the present Christian epoch.

APPENDIX
Is War Sin?

War is undeniably a social evil. A disposition, national or personal, to glory in mortal combat is of the devil (James 4:1, 2). War, however, is not an unmixed evil, or God would not have commanded wars to be initiated by his people. Furthermore, a sober view of history will find some good from settlement of international quarrels by war. It must be acknowledged, however, that most wars are both unnecessary and wrongfully motivated. Yet, *scripture never calls war, as such, a moral evil.* Hell is an evil also, but it is hardly demonstrable that hell is not a moral necessity. The necessity for such things as hell, jails, criminal courts, and war is where evil lies.

Let us not be *coerced* from debate by unsupportable, question-begging denunciations. If war were morally evil *per se,* I think we would not read of Michael and his holy angels at war with the devil and his angels; the military figures and symbols of scripture would be inappropriate. And certainly no text of the Bible would declare, "The Lord is a man of war: the Lord is his name" (Exod. 15:3). If war is sin, we may as well call the Lord a sinner.

"War is contrary to the will of God" is part of a long statement received at the First Assembly of the World Council of Churches at Amsterdam in 1948. Many pacifists of the time employed the statement to support their contention that war is sin. A respected figure among the supporters of the Assembly was Reinhold Niebuhr. Along with Angus Dun, Niebuhr published an article correcting the assertion. "As the context ought to make clear," they write, "this phrase is a condemnation of war as an institution, as a social evil. It does not say or mean that the aggressor and the victim are alike condemned" ("God Wills Both Justice and Peace," *Christianity and Crisis,* vol. 15, no. 10, June 13, 1955).

Niebuhr and Dun proceed to assert that (1) pacifism distorts the command of love; (2) it applies an individual ethic to a collective situation; and (3) the concept of a just war is defensible in means employed and ends sought, international law, and conscience. They allow that nuclear weapons now exacerbate the question of just war but do not essentially alter it.

CHAPTER 10
PEACE CHURCHES AND WAR POWERS

There is probably no aspect of peace-church doctrine more widely misunderstood than the teachings concerning the divinely ordained powers of government and the position of the Christian with regard to them. I already have had something to say about this; in this chapter we will essay to cover the subject more fully.

The earliest Anabaptist formal statement on the subject is Article 6 of the *Brotherly Union of a Number of Children of God Concerning Seven Articles,* commonly called *The Schleitheim Confession* (August 1527):

> *We hold that the sword is an ordinance of God, outside the perfection of Christ. Hence princes and authorities of the world are ordained to punish the wicked and to put them to death. But in the perfection of Christ, the ban is the heaviest penalty, without corporal death.*

This is how the Anabaptists wanted to state their endorsement of orderly civil government, including its police and war powers but without allowing themselves any form of participation in civil government.

Anabaptist groups have recently been immensely interested in finding out about the practices and doctrines of the early orthodox Anabaptists. Several fragments of the literature this has evoked are referred to in the notes at the end of this book. I will not discuss the literature as such, though I will seek to employ some of its contributions. The Anabaptists partially affirmed the state for the same scriptural and practical reasons all Christians have employed. Hans J. Hillerbrand summarizes their reasons for rejecting the state (i.e., "magistracy" or office-holding) for themselves: (1) lack of scriptural evidence; (2) the example of Christ; (3) the command of Jesus (as they interpreted Matt. 20:25–27); and (4) the sharp distinction between the church and the world.[1]

These arguments were reinforced then, as now, by something close to rejection of the Old Testament as authoritative on the Christian ethic for social living. The Anabaptists were (and still are) faulted by their opponents for this seemingly apparent deliberate act of limiting the sources of scriptural authority. All sorts of distinctions between letter and spirit, law and grace, and the like were brought to the debate. To the Anabaptists it seemed to matter little what the Old Testament said—texts relating to Jesus' words and example were sufficient for them.[2] Evidences as to the relevance or irrelevance of the texts were largely rejected out of hand as attempts to subvert the plain sense of scripture. Luther, Calvin (in his *Institutes* and *Commentaries*), and the successors of both were annoyed and baffled by the Anabaptists' behavior. Argument of any kind was largely futile.

Before long, Anabaptist missionary zeal waned and the movement came to be perpetuated largely by family descent as much as among Catholics, Reformed, and Lutherans. In the present century, however, several branches of Brethren and Mennonites have given their best human and material sources to foreign missions, to such an extent that their numbers on mission fields are nearly equal to those in the sending groups.

The nonresistance doctrines of the historic peace churches have undergone modifications in recent decades. It is hardly possible any longer to ascertain the stances of the present leaders and lay people of Mennonite, Hutterite, Amish, Church of the Brethren, and Brethren churches. As we have already observed from the books and articles of some who have moved toward theological liberalism, socialism, and other modernisms of our day, it appears that the views of many "Christian pacifists" are now practically indistinguishable from several kinds of pacifism that have no particular roots in historic Christianity.

Nevertheless, the historic peace churches do have some articulate exponents (or at least have had until very recently) who adhere closely to the traditions and who understand what those traditions are and what they mean. In this chapter we will consider what these "biblical pacifists" (as they sometimes call themselves) teach about the rightness of governments in waging war.

The peace churches do not assign enduring authority to creeds and statements. Thus none of the quotations that follow is fully comparable to creeds of "confessional" churches. Furthermore, in an age of change such as from 1940 to the present, the conference resolutions tend sometimes to be mere reformulations or simple repetitions of what the older ministers believe. (Those who disagree or who are undecided remain anonymous by remaining silent when these conference resolutions are put to vote.) The more conservative the group the more this is apt to be true, for the "fundamentalist" peace churches have most fully retained the orthodoxy of preceding centuries while making the most accommodation to current tides of evangelicalism.

There is little of either utopianism or perfectionist expectations among these down-to-earth, practical people. They are poles away from the various religious and secular pacifisms of our time, which care little for biblical roots. On these matters I quote the sound statements on the historic position by a modern-day orthodox Mennonite, John Drescher, of Eastern Mennonite Seminary:

> *Biblical pacifism is rooted in divine revelation and the necessity of new birth by the Holy Spirit. Its growth takes Scripture, Christ, and the church for sustenance; while other kinds of pacifism contain important truths, biblical pacifism is different in its orientation.*
>
> *Humanist pacifism places primary emphasis on what man can do, and applies a peace ethic to all society.*

Gandhian pacifism exerts pressure by peaceful means to accomplish deserved ends. Moralistic pacifism makes much of the immorality of war and dignity and goodness of man. Political pacifism proposes political action, law and pressure upon governments to avoid war. Anarchistic pacifism repudiates or rejects government. . . .

Biblical pacifism results from Christian discipleship. Refusal to fight is based on my calling as Christ's disciple. Jesus is Lord![3]

Through the years, people of Drescher's sort of persuasion have not tried directly to persuade governments one way or another regarding war. From time to time they have passed resolutions in their conferences condemning or commending this or that action of Presidents and Congress in the promotion of war or peace, but seldom—if ever—with heavy hand or strident voice.

They have usually regarded government as the business of others. They have felt that, as Christians, they were citizens of heaven with no right to impose the rules of heaven for themselves on the "governments of this world as being yet unregenerate" (see extract which follows).

A resolution of the National Conference of the Brethern Church in 1935 affirms and resolves, in part,

That we renew our historic position with relation to war; namely, that the Brethren Church from her origin has been utterly opposed to the use of violence or any physical force as a means to an end, on the part of the children of God. We regard the governments of this world as being yet unregenerate, and their methods of violence as contrary to the methods God has authorized His children in the present age to use. We reaffirm that war as a possible method for the attainment of justice, or the securing and maintenance of human liberty may at times be deemed necessary among the unregenerate of this world system, yet according to the teaching of our common Lord and Master we as His disciples do not belong to this world's system and its methods are not our own. We are in the world and not of it, as our Master taught (John 17:14), and

> *must maintain our pilgrim character (Heb. 11:8–16). We recognize and appreciate the protection of our flag of the United States. To the nation that God has ordained (Rom. 13:1–7) to afford us protection we gladly offer our services, time, money, and life itself, if necessary to bind up its wounds or to heal its sorrows, by any means or methods our Lord Jesus Christ has approved for the use of those who follow Him.*[4]

About five years after this resolution was passed, the president of the denominational seminary started publishing a periodical letter of counsel to the pastors and people on how to respond to the new universal conscription (draft) of 1940. A prominent "loyalist" pastor circularized the *Fraternity* (a relic of older antidenominationalism) with a summary of Brethren peace doctrine and excerpts from antiwar-nonresistance resolutions of the Brethren (Dunkers) from 1781 to 1940. The president's bulletins were so generally ignored (as was the pastor's circular letter) that the president quit sending them.

Few of the Brethren's eligible youth took the conscientious objector position. They simply marched off to the war as did their neighbors and schoolmates. I remember my own qualms of conscience about accepting the 4D (divinity students and pastors) classification.

But the Brethren did not give up. From time to time ministers and laymen convinced of the traditional nonresistance position would succeed in securing conference approval of resolutions and statements reasserting the "ancient faith." A statement of some length was prepared during the years 1942–1945. It affirmed the legitimate functions of *civil government* in local peacekeeping and in protecting the nation against its enemies. The commitment of these practitioners of nonresistance to the legitimacy of war by government *qua* government is clear and logical enough:

> *The Brethren Church clearly and gladly recognizes the divinely ordained place of civil government in a sinful world; that the government is truly a minister of God in the temporal realm for the purpose of protecting human*

life and "to execute wrath upon him that doeth evil." Therefore, the nation in exercising this divinely appointed function is authorized by the Word of God to "bear the sword" against evil-doers who may threaten the destruction of human life with its precious values of "justice" and "liberty." This divine authority and responsibility of civil government is clearly revealed in Scripture (Rom. 13:1–4), and has been recognized in former statements of the Brethren Church.

In the present situation, therefore, we should be ready to "be subject" to our government in every possible Christian way as set forth in Scripture (Rom. 13:5–7; 1 Pet. 2:13–14; Titus 3:1). This, we believe, includes the provision of funds [taxes] for the support and defense of the government in its divinely appointed work of protecting human life and executing wrath upon evil doers . . . (Rom. 13:6).

While fully recognizing the duty of the State to bear the sword against evil-doers, as sanctioned by the Scriptures, we also believe the same Word of God teaches that our personal ministry as Christian believers *should be exercised in spiritual matters and in the relief of human suffering, rather than in the taking of human life. As followers of Christ, citizens and ambassadors of His heavenly kingdom (Phil. 3:10,* ASV*; 2 Cor. 5:20), we are required by His Word to walk even as He walked (1 John 2:6; 1 Pet. 2:21–23) [that is, total non-use of physical force in any way; the ministry of suffering]. Therefore, we should be ready to serve our country in every possible way consistent with His Word, being willing, if necessary, to face danger and endure hardship in the performance of our duty, as long as we are not required to bear the sword personally in the taking of human life (John 18:36; Rom. 12:17–21; Matt. 26:52).*[5]

A great volume of similar material might be quoted. This group of Brethren goes farther than some Mennonites do toward approval of the coercive acts of government in local police and national wars. No genuine Mennonite or Dunker has ever taken the position of Tolstoy or of anarchists, who say the policeman sins in using force (they call it *violence*) to apprehend a violent criminal, and that war *per se* is sinful.

The statements quoted above declare in different ways that while it is just for sinful men to use physical force to enforce laws and to resort to wars in national defense (and many other just causes) it would be sinful for a Christian to do the same thing—every Christian is a citizen of the heavenly kingdom; the rules of that kingdom must take precedence over any human laws. Yet while advocating nonresistance they acknowledge that God's own "vengeance" is executed when the sword of civil government is employed. It is right for the policeman, soldier, executioner to take life for just reasons, but wrong for a Christian to be the policeman, soldier, or executioner? Is this paradox? *Antinomy*? It certainly does not qualify as biblical mystery. Is it illogic or even sheer contradiction?

The term *casuistry* refers to the application of a general ethical principle to a particular case of conscience or conduct. There is no area where the Christian advocate of nonresistance has more difficulty with his casuistry than in explaining why an action morally right for worldly government is morally wrong for believers, or, put the other way around, why something wrong for the believer is right for the unbeliever under the direction of worldly government.

The problem is not the same as explaining why what is wrong for a person in private capacity is right for one in civil (public) capacity. The mind easily finds many analogies for this distinction. For example, children do not chastise their parents, but parents their children; hired employees do not give orders to employers, but the other way around. Even more pertinently, while stockholders may elect the treasurer of their corporation, they are not permitted to write checks in payment of bills; only the treasurer or his designate may do so. The stockholders have no authority at all except in occasional stockholders' meetings, while the officers whom they choose exercise company authority at all times.

There is no analogy, however, to help explain the believer who may not use a weapon and the unbeliever who may justly do so.

In a lifetime of earnest search for an honest parallel among acknowledged, ethical human distinctions, I have come up empty-handed.

At this point the convinced religious pacifist may protest that the state has no authority to command anyone to do something that person holds to be a sin. But that argument will not work either, for the same person has already agreed that the suppression and punishment of evil by government and its officers is a positive good, however regrettable the necessity for such actions. Thus the pacifist's protests hedge at this point. Romans 13 always lurks nearby in all such protestations.

History, I think, demonstrates that this sort of argument requires another ingredient to be either logically coherent or practically successful. For want of a better name, I have called it social segregation. Up until fairly recent times, this ingredient has been a normal part of Mennonite and Dunker doctrine and practice.

Social segregation—or, as the older Anabaptist and Dunker writers preferred to say, "separation from the world"—was almost automatic in the early church. Believers who knew that Christ and he alone is Lord could not say also that Caesar is Lord (in a religious sense, that is). For two or three generations some Christians with rights of citizenship, of whom Paul is our paramount example, could claim a few civil liberties and the protections of Roman law. At Philippi, Corinth, Ephesus, and Jerusalem—to cite four examples only—Paul's Roman citizenship (at Philippi and Jerusalem) or the impartial application of Roman law by competent magistrates (Corinth and Ephesus) saved him from the attacks of unlawful mobs.

As time passed, though, these benefits of Roman law were lost for Christians—not invariably or constantly, but frequently. By the seventh decade of the first century, the profession of Christianity (demonstrated in court by refusal to pay religious homage to the symbol of Caesar) was in many districts a punishable crime. Christians were then outside the law—a nonpeople, not fit to receive the benefits of membership in Roman society. In such a situation, as we saw earlier, nonparticipation in military affairs was automatic. Christians were the frequent object of police action in a state where army and police were not fully distinct.

Later on the Empire became politically, economically, and militarily weak, while the Christian movement had become strong in numbers, reputation, and respect. Therefore the emperor declared Christianity *a* permitted religion; subsequently it was made *the only* permitted religion. After these developments it became the Christians' apparent duty not only to pray for the emperor but to come to his assistance. Christians now felt obliged to act as members of Roman society, exemplary members at that. Now it could no longer be said that they were only *in* the world [translate "society"]; they were also a part of it. This was an unfamiliar role to them. They could no longer maintain their "separation from the world" in any other sense than moral and spiritual excellence. If it was right for the officers and soldiers of government to bear the sword (Rom. 13) then it seemed right for a Christian to hold office as a member of society and, as an officer, to wield the governor's sword.

The problem of the Christians' relation to civil government arose in a similar way at the time of the Reformation. The Lutheran confessions of the sixteenth century support the dignity and rightness of the civil government as the *first use of the law.* Dietrich Bonhoeffer's *Ethics* (Part Two, I) clarifies the connection well and at length.[6] Calvin did his best to make the point with Anabaptists of his time.

This does not mean that the Christians of fourth-century Rome should not and did not use every channel open to them to work for peace. As Wolfhart Pannenberg has written, it was neither right nor possible after Christianity became permitted and then the only legal faith, for the Christians to separate themselves *en masse* from civil community. Some might privately pursue the older way, but it could not be universal among Christians. To fail to work for peace within the system of the civil commonwealth was to invite destruction of the civil order. Pannenberg writes,

> *As Christians assumed responsibility for political leadership in the Roman Empire, they could not long avoid the task of securing the internal peace of the empire against*

> *external threats, in spite of reservations about the compatibility of waging war and their position as Christians.*
>
> *This should not be regarded on principle and in each individual case as a departure from the spirit of the gospel,* unless we intend to forbid Christians to take part in political life at all. . . . *And Christians who as a matter of principle reject the dirty work of politics and the use of armed force find themselves in the ambiguous position of being beneficiaries of those who take such tasks on themselves on behalf of the entire society, and thus also on behalf of Christians [Roman mine].*[7]

Once it became a part of society, the ancient church did not give up its Christian witness. It was precisely at this juncture that the greatest theologian among the church fathers, Augustine of Hippo, composed the most profound and influential work on the subject of the church and the world. It was no capitulation to world-accommodation for Christians, but a theology for resistance to the sins of the world (the kingdom of Satan) by members of the Kingdom of God.

The European Anabaptists of Reformation times found themselves without civil rights largely because only one form of the Christian religion could legally be practiced by the permanent residents of any one of the numerous political units (states) of Europe. The idea of Christian denominations had not yet been born and it was almost universally believed that plurality of churches would undermine the fabric of social order. One could be evangelical (Protestant) in a land whose ruler was evangelical, or Catholic in a region whose ruler was Catholic, but not Protestant in a Catholic land or Catholic in a Protestant land. So there were thousands of migrations by people of conviction. The Anabaptists, who rejected the state-church idea, had no place to go except where they would be tolerated by either a Protestant or Catholic ruler. Holland was such a country; many emigrated to that land. Later some were invited to western Russia, where they formed communities of their own.

In 1648 the "wars of religion" were ended with a series of settlements collectively called the Peace of Westphalia. At this time the settling of America was in full swing. One of the colonies, Pennsylvania, was a "Quaker state" whose proprietor (William Penn) was a pacifist. For a long time the ruling class (Friends or Quakers) were religious pacifists, similar to the Anabaptists (Mennonites and Hutterites). A large number of the Mennonites migrated to Pennsylvania, as well as nearly all the Dunkers. In Pennsylvania these groups gave political support to the Quakers and went even so far as to enter the voting process, supporting the proprietor (Penn's family) and the Friends. This was a small breach of their separation-from-the-world stance, but it seemed allowable. During the Revolutionary War many internal conflicts arose in Pennsylvania, for conscientious objectors to military service were misunderstood.

As a part of their doctrine and practice, the Quakers observed the wearing of the plain clothes of the time of their origin. The Mennonites and Brethren (Dunkers) did not at first wear the special plain-clothes "uniform." Later, however, they did adopt the Quakers' custom of dress in order to show solidarity with the nonresistance stance of the Quakers.[8] These Mennonites and Dunkers became the "Pennsylvania Dutch"; a few of them are still known as such today. The later Anabaptist migrants, who came not to Pennsylvania but mainly to the prairie states and provinces of the United States and Canada, have not generally worn the peculiar costumes of the Pennsylvania Mennonites (including the Amish) and Brethren.

Now to the point of this brief historical excursion: these post-Reformation, nonresistance-separatists have been compelled by history to abandon their nonresistance and social separatism in some degree or other and in more than one way. Perhaps it is more generous to say they modified their position. The change has gone much farther. In some cases it can be shown that a complete reversal has taken place. The degree of modification, or even reversal, of the separatist-nonresistance stance has a general correspondence with the degree of integration into the society of the region where they live and by the degree to which they have penetrated the leadership of society. This has been documented by Mennonite and Brethren scholars, among others.

We have already noted that when the Unity of the Brethren (in Bohemia) began receiving lords of the realm into membership, their separatist-nonresistance was soon given up and before long they were involved in wars of self-preservation. The Anabaptists, though rejecting public office at first, found that in their Russian and Latin American communities congregational structure had to take on civil-public functions if orderly life was to go on. As noted earlier in the Netherlands, where they were first tolerated and accepted, the Mennonite Church became fully a part of Dutch life to the extent that a deacon of The Hague's congregation became a minister of the Dutch Navy. And in the U. S. the Church of the Brethren—traditionally a strong advocate of Christian noninvolvement in politics—reformed its stances considerably; during World War I one of its members (Martin G. Brumbaugh) became the governor of Pennsylvania.[9]

Mennonite and Brethren names are now prominent in the politics of the prairie provinces of Canada. The more conservative groups try to hold the line on the ancient customs and practices. But two tendencies away from the historic separatism and nonresistance doctrine are strong in all of them.

The first tendency leads toward accommodation and acceptance within the broad borders of North American evangelicalism. Brethren and Mennonites leaning in this direction are often led by ministers educated at independent, evangelical schools such as Biola, Moody, and Dallas, or even conservative denominational schools (Westminster, Trinity Divinity School, Grace Seminary). These Mennonites and Brethren listen to radio broadcasts such as "Back to the Bible" and "Day of Discovery" and read *Christianity Today, Evangelical Action,* and *Moody Monthly.* Independent faith missions have their share of missionaries of Mennonite and Brethren heritage. Their support of the ancient Anabaptist or Dunker heritage may be minimal, even nominal. Without specifically rejecting their distinct heritage, they are simply leaving their social separation behind. These groups tend to retain a fragment of their ancient nonresistance language in public statements, but the strict nonresistance of years past is all but dead. They furnish chaplains for the military, their young men usually cheerfully accept military conscription along with their neighbors, and many have advanced in the ranks of military service.

The second tendency among modern Mennonites and Brethren is away from the evangelical orthodoxy of their pietist ancestors toward doctrinaire pacifism and political activism. Some activists have added a program of statist socialism to their pacifism. Ronald Sider, cited earlier, wishes to be known as an evangelical, struggles manfully to make his arguments to square with scripture, and likes to drop the names of prominent evangelists and preachers as fellow-travelers in his journey. Sider overtly rejects the earlier social-political separatism of his Brethren denomination. The main project of his kind of Christianity is the establishment of peace and justice (that is, economic equality) in the world among all nations. This is no mere furtive induction from data in his writings, but is a constant emphasis. One meets the same political doctrines and statistics in Sider's *Rich Christians in an Age of Hunger* that are the bill of fare in *The New Republic* or in the more leftist articles in the Jesuit weekly, *America*.[10] *Rich Christians* is from start to finish an argument for socialism backed by national laws and, presumably, court enforcement.[11]

As we have seen, J. H. Yoder makes no bones about his departure from ancient norms and forms. Always respectful of the Anabaptist fathers and traditions, he nevertheless abandons them as well as much historically orthodox doctrine in general. For Yoder the gospel is a politico-social program of peace and socialism (that is, economic, social, and ethnic equalitarianism). He seems to be entirely at home with the Marxist formula: "From each according to his ability to each according to his need." Some have noticed that both Sider and Yoder would like to make the Mosaic law of redistribution of property every fifty years (the Jubilee) a sort of continuing formula for the political-social laws of nations. It appears they do not seek to enforce these laws through coercion (for both appear to be genuine pacifists) but through the church's adoption of the ideal of passive suffering. At least for Yoder, the gospel is the message of peace in the world and redistribution of goods and property.[12] Whether or not he intends to mix civil laws with such a gospel is not clear. The assembly of believers (i.e., the nonviolent, suffering group) is the demonstration and promotion center by which the program of peace and equality is to be brought to pass.

Yoder, along with his disciples and other religious pacifists of the past and present, would convert the old nonresistance doctrine into a principle of exemplary living. In Yoder's thought this principle is not merely a passive suffering such as one finds in 1 Peter 2:19–25. Yoder and his disciples want Christians to be active agitators for equality of goods and social benefits among men and, by providing in their churches a showcase for this Christian socialism, to be the harbingers of world peace and worldwide equality. The church at Jerusalem briefly practiced a limited form of voluntary sharing of goods, but there is not a trace of the Marxist or Jacobite social doctrines of "Liberty, Equality, and Fraternity."[13]

According to Yoder the church is to be a demonstration center and agitation center for these goals. He transforms the old nonresistance and separation principles into socialism and political pacifism. If taken literally, "Resist not evil" would have to include nonviolent resistance as well as violent resistance. But in the writings of this new breed of religious pacifists, the doctrine is changed from passivity to activity, from separation to involvement. They would be the avant garde of the transformation of society along pacifist and socialist lines. The peace churches no longer would be nonresistant pietist enclaves; they would be the harbingers of what sounds like a Tolstoyist or Marxist utopia.

11
THE CHRISTIAN'S SOCIAL RESPONSIBILITY

There is no way a person can more fully enter into the life of his people than to risk his life along with theirs in a war. As we have seen, several Christian groups have drawn the line against participation in the affairs of "the present evil world" short of getting involved in the military. While usually regarding government as ordained of God to restrain evil in society, they have regarded many things that government must do as dirty business.

Some Christians believe they should have nothing to do with oath taking, use of courts to settle disputes, holding public office, and even voting. Others have rejected not only government, but society as well.

All Christians acknowledge that, in certain respects, the world is indeed to be shunned. There is general disapproval of worldliness and excesses in pleasure and in accumulation of money and goods. There has always been a tendency for those of a certain temper to select a list of activities that place self-discipline or personal restraint at some stress and to label them as inherently worldly or sinful. If one does not do these things, they say, he is separated from the world.

No Christian can be quite without such rules. But the world the Bible warns against is a far more insidious tempter than are a few forbidden pleasures and indulgences. The warning in 1 John 2:15, 16 simply says, "Love not the world, neither the things that are in the world. If any man love the world, the love of the Father is not in him. For all that is in the world, the lust of the flesh, and the lust of the eyes, and the pride of life, is not of the Father, but is of the world." In some senses the whole world lies in wickedness (1 John 5:19). But the world is no sin except when it becomes an idol in the heart—not its silver and gold, sports and entertainment, even its nicotine, heroin and alcohol, its schools and theaters, its farms and fields, universities, courts, and markets. It is all a *cosmos* (the Greek word for "world" in 1 John 2), to which *cosmetic* is related (the Greek word for "adornment" in 1 Pet. 3:3). *Cosmetic* refers to a constantly changing arrangement or organization of things; it does not refer to the things themselves. After all, it is the same good, created order that was made for man's benefit and God's glory.

Since a wicked prince called Satan prevails in the world, it will always be misused for sin, even though the world sustains all our lives and is the scene of all Christian life and witness.

All people—good and bad—whom we meet in the pages of the New Testament were denizens of the world as it was arranged in the time of the apostles. Like the people of Jesus' parables and even in the days of Lot and Noah, they bought, they sold, they married, and procreated in the one world of those times.

Some of the very earliest post-New Testament Christian writers point out that Christians were in all regions of the Roman world. They were not distinguishable by the ways they earned their daily bread, by their dress, by their food and drink, nor by any special social organization, but by their *additional* association (church), their moral lives, and their love for one another. They had a beneficial effect on society precisely because they were *in* that society.

As Christians in society, is it wise, or even possible, to socially dissociate the Christian community from the general community in matters having to do with the actual conduct of society, things without which organized civilized life could not go on? As a matter of fact, we cannot. We may refuse the oath, but without it (or its legal equivalent) court processes are scarcely possible. We may refuse to hold office or vote, but if we do not, others must. We may refuse to be police officers, but if others do the same, our lives and property are unsafe. Wherever the Anabaptists set up their own semi-autonomous communities (as in Russia of two hundred years ago and recently in South America), the church itself had to assume these functions. Those first separatist English settlers, the pilgrims of Plymouth Colony, found it quite necessary to establish the same rudimentary instruments of civil government and societal process that they had left behind. No society can forego them for very long without reverting to civil disorder.

This being true, is it right or possible to want to be excused from the offices and tasks that as separatists we find unacceptable, while our very existence in society requires others to fill those offices and perform those tasks? Or, to put it otherwise (as it frequently is put), may I as a separatist clean the sewers as my service while my nonseparatist neighbor polices the streets; may I work in the hospital while my neighbor runs the courts and sits in the legislature? One of the church fathers said that Christian prayers did more good for the emperor than Christian military service could do. He may have been right. But did he choose the one to the exclusion of the other?

The separatist may say yes to each question above. If so, he will usually cite what has come to be known as "Peter's clause"—"We ought to obey God rather than men." Having cited this clause, however, it is incumbent upon him to prove that one is excluded from each social responsibility by a command of God. What Peter insisted upon was *not* that he should be excluded from a duty justly imposed on citizens, but that he had to proclaim the gospel of Christ, even if the civil officers of his community forbade him to do so. He would not be silent if God commanded him to speak. "We must not extract from this a general right to remain outside the prevailing legal system, even less the right to attack the political order actively."[1]

One may indeed withdraw on principle from many forms of voluntary association such as clubs, schools, labor unions, work forces, and the like. There are, however, involuntary associations and some voluntary ones from which men dare not withdraw and within which the members must perform their functions and duties. Furthermore, some relationships are grounded in creation or in the very foundations of society itself. They are natural, mutual associations. We may be in some of them unconsciously as well as involuntarily. These unbreakable relations are "orders" that exist before we are born and continue long after we die. As a noted Lutheran scholar has written, "They are orders which have validity in individual situations and whose existential orderliness always becomes apparent in the fact that they allow no substitution. A child cannot change place with his parents, or one marriage partner with the other. These individual orders are embedded in general orders which apply to all individual situations within a given category. Every child is required to honor only his parents, but all children in the world are subject to this general order because without parents there can be no children. What applies to one child applies to all."[2] There is no escaping the responsibilities of each person within the order. Some of the orders "claim us," this same scholar goes on to say, "without our explicit consent—our race, our national background, our citizenship. Nation and state occupy a special place in this connection because their existence exceeds the life span of the individual."[3]

In their best moments most people have insisted that the ethical thing to do when danger befalls their collective group (family, clan, nation) is to defend it. The pure pacifist says *no;* piety demands that he yield to aggression or, at the very least, to use no physical force to defend self, family, clan, or whatever. He suppresses natural love of family, clan, nation in the name of a principle—his own principle, though he may assert sincerely that it is a religious or Christian principle. The pure pacifist insists that the taking of a life through armed force is always wrong. In practice few pacifists have gone so far, but this is what pure (consistent?) pacifists say or certainly appear to say. They believe God can and does take life away from human beings—all of them, in fact—but he has no earthly surrogates.

Most Christians would certainly agree that God, the giver of life, has the right and power to take it away. God does not, however, give any man his life by fiat, "Let there be a new human life!" At the very moment of conception (and/or birth)

I am the creature of my parents who procreated me. I soon find myself also related by the extension of the procreative lines to grandparents, to ancestors long dead, to brothers and sisters, indeed to a whole extended family. My family is mutually obligated to neighbors, whose properties we have a duty to watch when they are away from home, and whose children and pets we seek to safeguard if they need it—not merely out of mercy and love, but out of justice and duty. No one in his right mind denies this. Further, all of us—family, clan and neighborhood—are protected by a political regime, which came into existence long before we were born. It keeps our roads open in winter, keeps crime in check, provides the public amenities that foster comforts and health, and promotes the general welfare.

All these societies (call them spheres, orders, or whatever) existed before I did. I entered them necessarily, simply by being born, and can scarcely escape them. I cannot replace parents in their rights and functions, nor the road commissioner, nor the district judge, nor the commander-in-chief of the country's defenses. Neither can any other human being exist in well-being without them.

In commenting on this state of affairs, Frederick D. Wilhelmsen, a professor of philosophy and politics at the University of Dallas (Irving, Texas), has written the following:

> *Whereas each concrete human being seeks his own perfection and happiness, his "particular good" . . . to the political order there belongs the quest for the common good. At the most basic level this common good is that of the family, sought by the head of a household. . . . [He proceeds to identify common good with* commonweal, *or well-being.]*
>
> *But "well-being" depends on "being." The pacifist doctrine, if widely spread, would simply have a political order surrender to enemies bent on its destruction. Pacifism is corporate suicide. By a curious irony a position that runs on the ticket of the sacredness of the life of the other ends up by denying [or appearing to do so] the sacredness of the lives of everybody within any society menaced in its very existence by hostile forces. I will not take his* life *by*

> *refusing to oppose him. Thus I connive in the murder of my fellow citizens and in the death of my own nation. Suicide is an indefensible action morally, but pacifism, in embracing corporate suicide, in effect borders on participation in murder. Putting the business in the form of the well-known paradigm of a man who refuses to defend his own family when attacked by thieves and potential rapists, we conclude ineluctably that he shares in the crime of his own aggressor.*[4]

It seems utterly reasonable that God-given office functions of nation and state, necessary for their continuance and the well-being of every citizen, are morally right—including police duties and national defense. The officer "beareth the sword," he is "the minister of God." But is it reasonable to suppose that Christian citizen-members of this "order" should try to *opt out* "for conscience sake" when they are directed to *support* the office and function "for conscience sake"?

As separatist believers assert, Christian discipleship requires us to model the regenerate, sanctified life by love and service. But it seems highly doubtful that this can be carried to the extreme of refusing actual duties established by divine law. I suggest that Christian discipleship might best be modeled *within* the office of soldier, magistrate, or policeman, precisely because there—in the crucible of life—the balance between God's justice on the one hand and his mercy on the other is placed in greatest prominence and in greatest strain.

It is impossible to achieve absolute separation from all cooperation in the necessary use of coercive force that government must use to perform its duties. There is no place to erect the division called "separation from the world" without apparent compromise. Even to enter a business or to sign a purchase agreement involves the sanctions of law, back of which are courts, magistrates, civil and criminal sanctions, and ultimately police, armies, and prisons—even war. The same goes for paying taxes or for obtaining a marriage license, an automobile registration, or a title deed to a piece of real estate.

The kind of separation from the world advocated by the older Anabaptists and by morally earnest evangelicals of many denominations today, may not really exist. It may just be impossible.

There is no consistency in refusal to be a part of civil government or in declining to endorse its task of restraining evil men, unless one goes beyond the Anabaptist position to Tolstoy's: to fight evil is sin; when the state fights against evil, the state as such *is* evil. Certain recent avant garde pacifists like to reinforce their positions by a bit of verbal magic. Drop the neutral word *force* and employ instead the pejorative word *violence*. The murderer then employs violence to kill a man and the policeman uses violence to apprehend and restrain the murderer. The murderer and the policeman are therefore equally evil. This manipulation of language is both unfair and perverse. It certainly merits the biblical woe upon those who "call evil good, and good evil" and who "put darkness for light, and light for darkness" (Isa. 5:20). Yet this seems to be the length to which some well-published pacifist writers wish us all to go.

CHAPTER 12
CHRISTIAN WITNESS TO THE STATE ABOUT WAR

The word *anarchy* is not, as sometimes supposed, a synonym for disorder, but there is a connection. Anarchy is the ancient Greek word for absence of government. Disorder and promiscuous, meaningless violence are the invariable consequences of the absence of the plain, visible hand of civil government.

There is a whole book of the Bible largely given over to the story of the disorders of ancient Israel in a period of several centuries when there was no clear civil power over all the tribes even though there was a measure of unity of religious practice and a common central sanctuary—a sort of "amphictyonic league." This is the Book of Judges, which in Hebrew really means "Rulers." The last verse of the book reads, "In those days there was no king in Israel: every man did that which was right in his own eyes" (Judg. 21:25). The times were disorderly because there was no orderly succession of rulers in Israel. Anarchy does not consist of disorder; it is the cause of disorder.

The Bible represents the period before the Flood of Noah as a period without civil governments. The Bible reports the results of this unlimited freedom of men to do what they would: "Now the earth was corrupt in God's sight, and the earth was filled with violence. . . . And God said to Noah, 'I have determined to make an end of all flesh [i.e., of the human race]; for the earth is filled with violence through them'" (Gen. 6:11, 13, RSV).[1]

Evidently there was no hope of taming such worldwide mayhem, so God removed the mortal population a bit early and started over with a select, regenerate (though sinful) group of four married couples. And, as a distinct new feature of the new order, he instituted civil government (see Gen. 9:1-7).

From then to now few thoughtful people—whether Jewish, pagan, Christian or otherwise—have doubted that civil government is essential to organized society. Life and limb, practice of industry and art, conduct of family life, and orderly religion depend upon governments' performing their divinely given function with a decent degree of faithfulness.

What is not obvious, except through biblical revelation, is that civil government was specifically given by God as a partial social remedy for sin. There have been several alternate views: (1) man's nature is completely fulfilled only in a civil state of some kind; or (2) as a matter of utility in primitive times, people imposed upon themselves a "social contract" to be ruled by a few for the good of all; or (3) in the evolution of the social classes, certain power classes (bourgeoisie) by violence and persuasion have subdued the lower classes (proletariat) to work and to obey.[2] There may be glimmerings of truth in each of these three best-known alternatives to the common Reformation-Protestant view endorsed here. Each is either false or inadequate as a ground for civil government. In a world ordered by God, authority must not simply be assumed or accepted unless God, the Lord of all, grants it. It is abundantly clear in scripture that civil government is God's own invention. God has ordained civil government and imparted to its magistrates the "power of the sword." That is, magistrates have the right and duty to coerce civil order by physical force, if necessary even to wage war: "There is no power but of God: the powers that be are ordained of God" (Rom. 13:1); "Thou couldst have no power at all against me, except it were given thee from above" (John 19:11); "Rulers are not a terror to good works, but to the evil" (Rom. 13:3).

Paul's acceptance of this state of the matter is reflected in his words to a Roman magistrate: "If then I am a wrongdoer, and have committed anything for which I deserve to die, I do not seek to escape death; but if there is nothing in their charges against me, no one can give me up to them. I appeal to Caesar" (Acts 25:11, RSV). All the essential features of orderly, coercive civil government are there implied and endorsed by the greatest of the New Testament doctrinal authorities. We shall shortly return to this subject.

It is important to note in this connection that the Bible accepts warfare as a fact of life, not disapproved *as such* by the writers nor in any way condemned *as such* by God. The first account of a war in scripture is a raid for purposes of plunder by a rapacious consortium of four large kingdoms against five small kingdoms at the edge of Canaan (see Gen. 14). Two of the small kingdoms were the most famous in all literature for sin and corruption of every kind, Sodom and Gomorrah. In this war Abraham, the sainted progenitor of the Hebrew people, entered in a decisive way, though his interests were not in who won but in the safety of his nephew's family and in the preservation of their properties.

Like every human endeavor, the preservation of order and promotion of public welfare by government has been accomplished with much less than a steady pursuit of justice. Scripture makes clear that God himself is the real king of all the earth. He loves the human race, whom he created for his glory, and will not cease his governance thereof until all his purposes in redemption are accomplished. In his rule of the world, war has a place.

At this point we ought to take note of several pertinent teachings:

1. Nothing is ever going to destroy either the human race or the natural order essential to its existence until the consummation of redemption. God will destroy all his enemies and humankind's, including death: "The last enemy to be destroyed is death" (1 Cor. 15:26, RSV). In the interval, we have God's promise, "I will never again curse the ground because of man, for the imagination of man's heart is evil from his youth [severe punishments do not extirpate inborn sin]; neither will I ever again destroy every living creature as I have done. While the earth remains, seedtime and harvest, cold

and heat, summer and winter, day and night, shall not cease" (Gen. 8:21, 22, RSV).

2. God is the providential ruler of the world, "the one in charge." Bible readers never need to be convinced that such is its teaching. God is the "judge of all the earth"; this is the theme of Psalms 92–99. "There is no power but of God" (Rom. 13:1). He uses various means of control—sunshine, rain, and "fruitful seasons" as well as famines, pestilences, earthquakes, and floods. Sometimes he sends evil times and dissolute, cruel rulers to restrain men's sins; sometimes good rulers and peaceful times in response to prayer or for purposes known only to him.

3. Some of the measures taken by God can be very severe. War is one of those measures. He creates the desolations of war by his providence as well as the blessings of peace. On a summer day in 1945, with Japan in humiliating defeat and much of Europe in ruins, with millions of the recently dead freshly buried, and with millions of continental European peoples displaced, I preached a V-E Day sermon at a community gathering in Indiana. My text was Psalm 46, part of which reads, "The nations rage, the kingdoms totter; he utters his voice, the earth melts. The Lord of hosts is with us; the God of Jacob is our refuge. Come, behold the works of the Lord, how he has wrought desolations in the earth. He makes wars cease to the end of the earth; he breaks the bow, and shatters the spear, he burns the chariots with fire! 'Be still, and know that I am God. I am exalted among the nations, I am exalted in the earth!'" (Ps. 46:6–10, RSV). The application of the psalm to the history of 1939–1945 is obvious.

If we truly want to follow assessments of the place of war in God's providential actions in history, there is an abundance of material to draw on. The war by which Joshua's armies conquered Canaan was one of divine justice: punishment of the Canaanites for their corrupt way of living and of worshipping their gods. They were allowed four final centuries of grace (Gen. 15:13, 14) which they might have used to reform and to escape annihilation; but they only became riper in their deserving of divine judgment. In a remarkable case of historical symmetry, about a millennium later the Israelites who replaced them were evicted for the same sorts of sins.

Scripture says the very ground vomited out the Israelites in disgust and outrage against their unpunished, unrequited sins (Lev. 16:25-28; 2 Chron. 36:14-18).

Some of the new-breed peace-church activists are correct in reminding us that there are worse things than loss of national sovereignty and forced submission to foreign conquerors. However, they speak in this way to encourage abandonment of national defenses—unilateral disarmament of the West. They get a hearing only in free countries. Their books are not sold in China and the Soviet Union. They are nevertheless correct in part, for it is better that a nation of Christian profession or of any decent moral standards have its sins punished, its corrupt tendencies stayed, and its rampage to dissolute living halted by any means God chooses, than that its peoples continue a headlong plunge to perdition.

4. Where Christians are allowed to speak, they have much indeed to tell their rulers about the justice and piety that God—the ruler of nations—encourages and requires. As to the subject of war, what they have to say will inevitably take some form of what has come to be called "just war" doctrine.

Moral philosophers of the Middle Ages gave a number of criteria by which to judge "just cause" for a war. Of course, there is a certain irony in the fact that the wars of the Middle Ages were mainly among nations of Christendom. The criteria are six: that the war be waged (1) by a lawful government; (2) for a just cause; (3) with proper intent; (4) with due consideration of advantages and disadvantages; (5) with means that are compatible with the nature of the conflict [not with excessive use of force]; and (6) with recognition of the distinction between combatants and noncombatants.[3] (See appendix on page 127.)

J. G. Davies, a British writer, recites these six principles of just war doctrine at much greater length, then states that this doctrine "has provided a basis for moral discrimination and for moral objections to specific wars. Without facing these questions with the assistance of such a theory, Christians would be opting out of history; they would be denying their traditional view that political society is necessary for human good on earth, and they would have simply nothing to say of any relevance in those situations where wars may obtain."[4]

There have always been some Christians who, to use Davies' words, have opted out of history and simply left the business of government and of war to those who frequently enough have had no conscientious scruples at all. Most, however, at least from Augustine's time until now, have participated in civil life. We do not need to defend or excuse all that professed Christians have done as citizens or soldiers any more than any one of us will attempt to defend or excuse ourselves at the judgment. But in all ages Christians have had a basis in moral conviction for what they did as citizens in armed service of their country. This basis has always been some form of what is now called "just-war" doctrine.

It is strange that Augustine frequently should be credited with inventing the Christian "just-war" idea. In his view none of man's works is just (righteous). The problem has arisen from the translation of the Latin nouns *jus* and *justitia* and the adjective *justus, a, um*. The *justum bellum* of Augustine probably should be translated "*justified* war," not "just war."

In Augustine's opinion, guided by Paul's epistles, all mankind is sinful. Individually and collectively they are corrupt, culpable, and guilty. Hence, the pride of man "hates the fellowship of equality under God, and seeks to impose its own dominion on fellowmen, in place of God's rule. This means that it hates the just peace of God, and loves its own peace of injustice. And yet it cannot help loving peace of some kind or other."[5] If, as Augustine asserts, the very best peace of the "City of the World" is unjust ("the tender mercies of the wicked are cruel"), then its so-called just wars are unjust, too. But this should not cause Christians, every one a sinful man justified by grace, to reject the idea of justified war.

In *The City of God* there is a passage wherein Augustine points out that language differences are a great divider of men and remarks that one "would be more cheerful with his dog for company than with a foreigner" (Augustine was not a language scholar). Rome, he says, cured some of this evil by creating a large empire and imposing a single language on it. Yet he deplored the past slaughter and noted that even more bloody civil wars within the empire disquieted mankind. Then he goes on to remark that "they say" wise men will wage only "just wars." He admits this reluctantly, granting that injustice can be severe enough to require wise leaders of men to wage war. It is something, Augustine says, that anyone cannot even think about without pain, if he remembers that he himself is also a human being.[6]

The justified war teaching is no formula for conducting simon-pure wars of no moral ambiguity. Sin manages to pervade all things human. Even theological faculties and church committees exist under the condition of sin. In this sense, there is not even one just Christian missionary society or evangelistic effort. These facts render Christian just(ified)-war teachings realistic. They should not be judged by a standard of perfection demanded of nothing else in the area of human conduct.

By piecing together passages from several of his writings, we know Augustine's idea of a justified war would be (1) a war to defend justice; (2) motivated by love even for the enemy [how does a *government* love anything?]; (3) conducted without unnecessary violence; and, most important, (4) waged only by the authority of rulers, not of private persons.

These and other principles have been discussed by Christian moral philosophers through the centuries. Catholic writers refer often to enlargements by Thomas Aquinas (1225-1274). In an important passage Aquinas asserts that three things are necessary if a war is to be a just one: (1) it must be waged by the authority of some recognized sovereign power [he seems to acknowledge no just revolutions]; (2) there must be a just cause for an attack—those who are attacked must deserve to be attacked; and (3) belligerents must act with right intentions, intending either advancement of good or avoidance of evil.[7]

Protestants refer to Hugo Grotius (1583-1645), a Dutch statesman and writer, but he is rarely quoted in present discussions. Arthur F. Holmes of Wheaton College has made a significant portion of Grotius' views available in his *War and Christian Ethics* (Grand Rapids: Baker Book House, 1975, pp. 226-238). All the Protestant leaders of the era of religious wars ending in 1648 (except in Britain) were vitally concerned with a Christian theology for just insurgency or revolutionary wars against oppression. There are many current writers, chiefly Roman Catholic and Latin American, who have sought to turn the just-war teaching into a doctrine of Christian armed revolution, or liberation theology. This effort will have to stop short of the subject of the possible justification of armed revolution.

The doctrine of just war (that is, of war limited by moral principles) finds considerable specific support in the Judaeo-Christian sources, beginning with the Hebrew Scriptures.

The seemingly exceptional case of annihilation of the Canaanites, Midianites, and others in the initial conquest of the Promised Land may cause us to forget that ordinarily the Old Testament supports limitations on allowable destructive force in any war. In the first two chapters of Amos, five neighbors of Israel and Judah are cited for divine judgment. The causes in each case involve flagrant breaches of what today might be called a civilized code of war. Damascus had used unnecessary brutality against Gileadite civilians in a war raid (Amos 1:3); Gaza had unnecessarily dispossessed a whole people of their territory (1:6); Tyre had done the same and had broken a solemn diplomatic covenant (1:9); Edom had taken the sword in unjustified hatred and anger against a neighbor nation and refused to stop (1:11); Ammon had committed atrocities against defenseless pregnant women with no greater cause than desire to enlarge territory (1:13); Moab had committed sacrilege, wantonly desecrating the national cemetery of the kingdom of Edom (2:1). There is no previous word of scripture addressed to these heathen nations on the subject of civilized conduct of war. These standards must arise in man's awareness simply because he is man. One may call this natural light, or natural law. These passages in Amos tacitly assume a doctrine of limited (just) war, to which the God of the Bible is committed and for which he holds all nations responsible.

Several of the books called Latter Prophets by Jews and Major and Minor Prophets by Christians have large sections addressed to the nations of antiquity—neighbors of Israel near and far. These sections have extensive teachings on the subject of justice and injustice in war. Some of the teachings are (1) that God may use the armies of a very wicked nation to judge a less wicked one; (2) that the pagan emperors and generals are unaware of their service to the divine Lord of the world as instruments of his judgments; (3) that godly people must be prepared to experience the sufferings incident to the judgments God inflicts by warfare on their wicked fellow populace; (4) that armaments of defense are of no avail for defense if God has determined destruction; and (5) that armaments of aggression against a people are of no avail if God has determined deliverance. The historical portions of the scriptures lavishly illustrate all of these principles.

All of these traditional biblical teachings and precedents have gone into the doctrines of the churches about the "just" or "justified" war. They have not been without good effect. Christianization of societies has improved them in many ways but never perfected them. People who expect perfection in this life will have to settle for less until the Kingdom of God comes. In like manner, while war has never been eliminated within Christendom, Christian just-war doctrine has greatly relieved warfare of terrors. The extreme cruelty of war among peoples of the Far East was shocking to Americans and Europeans during World War II, but the Chinese and Japanese had no Christian, just-war doctrine or sentiment. International laws of war have grown up almost wholly on the soil of Christendom.

As history shows, Christian restraints have alleviated suffering of innocent noncombatants and reduced wanton destruction. Popes and bishops frequently admonished and rebuked rulers who broke the code. Regrettably, even in epochs of intense religious feeling in European Christendom the unnecessary cruelties of war have never quite been put to an end, even though preservation of lives of prisoners, respect for noncombatant civilian population, and the like have been commonly followed. The Thirty Years War (ended 1648) left much of Europe with sharply reduced populations and desolated countrysides. Yet everyone involved in this great Catholic versus Protestant war was pledged to some form of a Christian doctrine of just war. Even so, one must ask, How much worse would the results have been if there had been no teaching to restrain the wantonness of weary soldiery and the desperate policies of rulers?

Lack of complete adherence to rules and restraints in commerce, marriage, traffic, and use of property, does not mean that the rules are not necessary to civilization. Christian men and women are in error when they expect perfect bliss in marriage. But that does not mean the marriage should be abandoned. Rather, good sense requires only that expectations from marriage should be realistic. What more can be expected of nations?

Yet, having said all this, it must be acknowledged that even before the world wars of our century there have been few causes which justified the terrible wars we read about in our history books. In retrospect, and in far greater possession of all the facts than the participants of long ago, we find it difficult even now to know exactly which were just. Leaders always seek to justify their causes before their constituencies and, to a lesser extent, before the world. Every situation seems to be unique. It seemed so very noble to war against the Turks four centuries ago, scarcely less than against the Kaiser in 1914–18, or against Hitler in 1939–45, or against the perpetrators of the "day of infamy"—December 7, 1941. Yet the passing of time, while not exactly changing many verdicts, puts those conflicts in different lights.

A. A. Hodge of Princeton was a well-respected defender of the just-war doctrine, but he also wrote, "War is an incalculable evil, because of the lives it destroys, the misery it occasions, and the moral degradation it infallibly works on all sides . . . vanquished . . . victor . . . the right . . . and the wrong."[8] He condemned most of the real causes underlying decisions to go to war and suggested some guidelines for such decisions—none of which is ever likely to be considered in the U.S. Senate in contemplating a declaration of war.

Nevertheless, if a nation is Christian—even in the least possible sense—the leaders ought not to offend its people by sponsoring unnecessary wars. They should not seek to compel or enlist them to fight in palpably unjust war adventures.

Jesus said there would be wars and rumors of wars, and Daniel prophesied that wars are determined to the end. Yet neither intended to lend any support to a love of conflict and of bloodshed by civil and military leaders. Many prophets discouraged kings from embarking on needless wars. Some even encouraged surrender to the enemies of the covenant nation. There is no general scriptural formula to determine when a nation should or should not engage in war. In the Bible, while war *as such* is not wrong, many of the wars are judged as futile and unnecessary.

What shall we say of the wars our own family traditions recall, of the wars our history books narrate? Some of the wars have indeed settled great issues and were followed by lengthy seasons of peace. Aside from God's providence, wars as instruments of national policy are decided by power, not justice. Justice, real or alleged, is the published ground on which leaders proceed. As I review the early wars of my country, how little they now seem necessary! Canadians tend to think of the American Revolution as reckless and unnecessary—taxation without representation a pretext, not a just cause.

Who now can say our southern states had no ground in justice to secede? Were the results, beyond preservation of the Union, prevailingly just?

Are we too close to our wars of the present century to evaluate them fairly?[9]

APPENDIX
On Just-War Theories

Writers on Christian just-war doctrine do not state the six principles (page 121) in the same manner. Sometimes "probability of success" is added as a seventh. War should not be initiated if nothing is to be gained. It is wrong to make a futile gesture of war. This principle can be found in the Book of Jeremiah, where surrender is advocated in face of certain destruction otherwise. Distinction can be made between just cause of war (*jus ad bellum*)—to which the six or seven principles above apply—and just conduct, i.e., actions, strategy, tactics (*jus in bello*). In the latter case—conduct of war—the principles of just cause and several more apply.

The 1983 Pastoral Letter of the Roman Catholic Bishops of the United States attempts to apply the just-cause principle of "appropriate means" (or, as the bishops would have it, "proportionality") to make their case against possession of nuclear weapons. They also refer to a just-conduct principle of "discrimination."

The bishops have assembled an impressive case, which may have effect until a serious crisis or threat comes along. Then, the world of sinful men being what it is, our leaders will simply do what they think they have to do. Then the wisdom of E. L. R. Long will apply:

> *The several criteria for determining the justice of any particular war constitute an imposing array of insight and analysis. They specifically endorse the use of armed coercion to maintain or to establish conditions of peace and justice while at the same time implying limits upon the legitimate exercise of military force. However, just-war teaching has been more impressive on the theoretical level than significant in qualifying or halting particular wars. Even those who agree on principle can argue in particular cases whether all possible solutions short of conflict have been exhausted, whether military operations protect more than they destroy, and whether humane restraints against wanton destruction have been observed. To say, therefore, that a particular war is "just" is to describe the judgments made about it by a particular individual or a particular group and not to report an objective condition concerning which all observers agree. There have only been wars that some men have considered just and wars that some men have considered unjust.* (*War and Conscience in America*, Philadelphia: Westminster, 1968, p. 31)

The author adds correctly that the criteria were formulated by Christians to explain to themselves how they could obey rulers—even *pagan* rulers—in going to war. There was never full agreement that they could support rulers even in unjust causes.

The leaders of the Roman Church changed the ethic of war to a new foundation during the Crusades. Now war was to be regarded as a just instrument for achievement of success in a cause, to recover the "holy places" from custody of unbelievers. A modern slogan such as, "Make the world safe for democracy" rests on such an ethical theory.

To attempt a full survey of all views of the ethics of war through the centuries is a larger project than can be undertaken here. A very helpful book edited by Arthur F. Holmes of Wheaton College gathers together some of the most important writings, from Plato to Paul Ramsey, with a short introduction to each (*War and Christian Ethics,* Grand Rapids: Baker Book House, 1975). Holmes' own exposition of just-war doctrine appears in a very attractive essay in *War: Four Christian Views,* edited by Robert G. Clouse (Downers Grove, Ill.: Inter-Varsity Press, 1981).

CHAPTER 13
NUCLEAR "PACIFISM"

Pacifism appears in quotation marks in the chapter heading because many, if not most, of the sincere people who are putting up arguments for nuclear disarmament or a "nuclear freeze" are not pacifists at all. They are influenced specifically by the "nuclear terror," quite apart from any convictions about armies and navies and the duties of governments. They want armed policemen to patrol their area of residence and their rulers to stand up to enemy nations. They are advocating a new and special limit on war; thus implicitly they are supporters of a just-war doctrine.

Most doctrinaire pacifists insist that war is not only a social evil, but sin. Thus the consistent, honest pacifist will not be found arguing against nuclear arms on the practical grounds (destructiveness, expense, etc.) which certain members of Congress or the Roman Catholic bishops have used to advocate that nuclear arms be outlawed, reduced, or "frozen." The genuine pacifists ought to stay out of this argument with their "hidden agenda" for the same reason that Protestant ministers should be silent at Roman Catholic clergy retreats or Republicans at a Democratic political caucus.

Religious and philosophical pacifists have, however, entered furiously into the campaign to bring about in one degree or another the elimination of nuclear arms from the arsenal of the United States and other NATO countries. Their arguments, of course, are not published on the other side of the Iron Curtain. With some allowance for oversimplification, the arguments they passionately bring forward, some as if there were no possibility of doubt or refutation, are chiefly five:

1. The invention of nuclear weapons has changed completely the rules of nations for conduct of war. Any war between major powers which can and will use nuclear weapons puts the entire human family at risk. So any threat by one of these powers must simply remain unopposed, for to oppose it might "trigger nuclear war," which would certainly be escalated to world-destroying proportions.

2. There is no such thing as victory of one nation or alliance against another in nuclear war. (These pacifists allow no distinction between refined weapons free of fallout designed to attack military personnel and installations and the "dirty" mass-destruction weapons of thirty years ago.) It is simple waste of effort and money to attempt victory. Everybody loses and loses utterly.

3. However defined, there can no longer be any such thing as a just (or justified) war. Preservation of humanity must now be the stance of everyone. The distinction between *good* and *bad* ones is out of date, if it ever was valid.

4. Since the fifties pacifists and others have argued that in view of the above "facts," nations and national governments may now be the chief obstacles to the peace of the world. What the world needs is a world government with a world police force to make the *peoples* behave. (This sounds remarkably like saying that the chief cause of cancer is people contracting it: "We really ought to eliminate people so there would no longer be any danger of cancer.") What is most surprising is that this view of things has been issuing steadily from church conferences, pastoral letters, and religious resolutions committees—not least the documents of Vatican II. The Bible refers to one such effort at one-world government—the Tower of Babel incident of Genesis 11. It also speaks of the future worldwide reign of the Antichrist and of the future universal kingdom of Christ.

5. The thousands of people who demonstrate against nuclear power plants, sometimes in the alleged cause of a clean

environment, often state their case as if all nuclear forces, peacefully employed or otherwise, are inherently evil. The same reasoning would eliminate almost every invention since the foundation of the world, beginning with mortar and pestle, for who could prevent the use of either or both to smash someone's head?

There are many obstacles to reasonable debate about the ethics of nuclear arms possession and proliferation. Among them are the following:

1. A great deal of obscurity caused by the growing number of unexplained technical terms that the participants direct at one another.
2. Very technical data about nuclear arms and deployment appearing in quite *un*technical popular forums of debate.
3. Hysteria and sloganizing, rather than reason, among the most vocal and publicized participants in the contest.
4. Lack of precise, verifiable information about the effects of nuclear weapons when used. Are the effects what some scientists say? Are they worse than the effects the new "conventional" weapons produce? Experiments are not possible and we have treaties against them.
5. Persistence of all sorts of unverified claims and counterclaims—apart from reasonable projections.
6. Fear inspired by the mysterious, unprecedented horror a nuclear war would wreak.

These are only some of the obstacles to clear-headed discussion. Let us address some of them before attending to some proposals.

First, the enlarging vocabulary jargon: words, phrases, and nuances of "nuclearspeak" have increased mightily through the nearly forty years the problem has been with us. In the summer of 1945 it was only *atomic bomb* and *atomic fission*. Soon arrived *hydrogen bomb, nuclear fission, nuclear fusion, fallout,* and the like. And now look what has happened to the language of nuclearspeak! A single one-sixth page newspaper article, by Thomas J. Bray[1] furnished seventy unfamiliar words, phrases, and nuances peculiar to this new department of discourse. A single sentence gives the flavor: "He deftly explains such arcana as game theory, systems analysis and Standard Integrated Operational Plans." A few words are self-explanatory new expressions, such as *anti-nuclear activist, more moral defense,* and *anti-technical,* which relate more to the verbal conflict over nuclear weapons than to the weapons themselves. Deeper into the debate are familiar words with new meanings or nuances: *yield of weaponry, counterforce, dirty weapons, stabilizing weapons, radiological, massive retaliation, flexible response strategy,* and many more. Then there are still more technical terms, names of participants in the debate, and obscure references to thirty-five years of prior discussion, all of which have to be learned to enter the main stream of the discussion on nuclear war: *nuclear genie,* ABM, RAND Corp., *counterforce and countervalue,* Herman Kahn, Manhattan Project. No wonder most people (except when the periodic waves of nuclear *angst* have peaked) have been content to leave the whole matter in the hands of scientists, diplomats, and the Pentagon.

We must also consider an obstacle of a different order: the frame of mind of the generations most involved in the discussion—people twenty to sixty years old. In America this corresponds roughly with the television age, unparalleled comfort, ease, and education, growing freedom of expression and movement, plus good health care. The ancient threats of famine, pestilence, and epidemics are muted, out of sight, or perhaps conquered. Death is one intractable enemy which cannot be indefinitely avoided, but we have even learned how to make funerals at least outwardly beautiful. In this kind of society, peace and comfort seem to be normal. For the most part, somehow we manage even to ignore drunk driving and violent crime.

With this common frame of mind, today's generations cannot willingly accept the fact that the same technical science that has created our semi-utopia has also, in the invention of atomic fission and nuclear fusion, produced the human means of its own destruction. People simply do not want to look at this paradox of modern life; so when compelled to look at it, many respond with anger, frustration, or hysteria. Christians ought by all means to respond with the knowledge and measured judgment of biblical doctrine and prediction.

We must formulate some reasoned responses to a new problem that affects the whole human race.

It is probably true that in our land some sort of democratically attained consensus must prevail. A few Christians are drawn by the almost hallowed mystery of nuclear devastation, an element that seems to tap into the very subsistence of the universe of God (see Rudolf Otto's *mysterium tremendum* and *mysterium fascinosum*). Most of us Christians, however, remain simply unmoved or even repelled. Come election time we vote our present mood, prejudices, past information, misinformation, hearsay, or even the unverified claims and counterclaims of those who shout the loudest. But this must change; Christian people must now become informed and furnish some leadership.

The way we approach the problem posed by nuclear weapons and warfare seems to be no different from the way we ought to approach other problems of Christian response to public issues. In common with biblical Christians everywhere, we already know that in a world of sinful men God raised up civil governments to place restraints upon oppressive, rapacious, and violent actions of men and their various collectives, from robber bands to armies of the nations. Roman Catholic moral philosophy traces the mandate of civil government to natural law rather than to biblically revealed mandate, but it agrees in the result: "the powers that be are ordained of God." Therefore we will support the right and duty of our rulers to use necessary means to secure the necessary goal of defending our country and our neighbors who cannot defend themselves against international bullies. We must also use every insight, and every rightful channel of influence to help direct those means wisely and well.

So we must reluctantly acknowledge that war, though often pursued mindlessly with unnecessary brutality, perhaps even by our own forces, is a necessary means of carrying out the necessary duties of a government. However, the utterly destructive nature of nuclear weapons (and of recent "conventional" weapons that approach the destructive ferocity of nuclear weapons) forces us to consider other factors. We have all heard statistics and projections about the probable results of detonating, in a few fierce exchanges, all such weapons in the world—however unlikely such a course of events might be. The question that faces us, then, is this: Does a biblical Christian (or just-war) doctrine require us to oppose armament with nuclear weapons?

The world lives under a sustained threat of widespread, unprecedented devastation. The worst is that, until some of these devices are detonated, we will have to imagine what the results might be. Our imaginations have been aroused by unending waves of stimulation by the testimony of scientists, as well as by novels, movies, articles, and TV specials. Rather than to exercise more imagination, we might profitably look deep into the past to understand what discerning people thought when the breakup of the ancient world seemed to be, and truly was, imminent. Commenting on one of the dozens of ruined ancient cities he had examined, W. R. Ramsey said that when the ancient world of Greece and Rome perished, it perished utterly. We cannot now imagine what the breakup of the Roman Empire meant to Italy and North Africa. Saint Augustine's *The City of God*, composed while the catastrophe was taking place, shines through the ages as an example of Christian adequacy for the moment, however shocking the moment might be. Says Michael Novak,

> *From biblical times, the human race has often been warned that God might will or permit its destruction. When Cain slew Abel, he prefigured the possibility of threat to all the progeny of Adam and Eve, including himself, for by the same passion he might have slain not only his brother but also his parents and finally himself. In the story of Noah, the Bible instructs us in the image of the destruction of the whole world by flood, and warns us of God's threat to destroy all the world by fire. Sodom, Gomorrah, and other cities were utterly destroyed in vivid biblical warning, as was the temple at Jerusalem. To live under the threat of flood, fire, glacier, plague, pestilence, war, and destruction is not novel for an imagination attuned to biblical history. The destruction of Carthage, the levelling of the glories of Greece and Rome, and the coming night of barbarism inspired St. Augustine to oppose secular millenarianism and a false sense of catastrophe [i.e., a false*

sense of doom), as he penned The City of God. *The ruin of civilization is not a theme new to our time, nor is the theme of destruction of all things living. Since Jewish and Christian conscience has long been steeled by contemplation of the fragility of this world and the overpowering sovereignty of God, our generation should not separate itself too dramatically from all others. The prophecies of the Book of Revelation (see chapters 8 and 9) exceed even the horrors of the twentieth century.*[2]

It is wise to bring as much biblical truth about the world and its history as we can muster to the prospect of immense destruction of civilization within our lifetime. After we have heard the experts recount the worst possible nuclear devastation, we are compelled to recover the biblical teaching about the perilousness of all life on this earth, the temporary quality of all earthly possessions, the end of the present age in divine judgment, and the beauty and glory of eternal life with God. Though the world is a good creation of God, it is inhabited by an obdurately and perpetually wicked human race. But God is in charge and will bring it all to a successful consummation. No situation is without rhyme and reason if God truly is in control, and he is. Nuclear weapons have changed much in the world, but they cannot alter the fundamentals of the Christian world view: that we live in a cosmos—not a chaos—and that God planned the world, created it, sustains it, governs it, and will guide it to his goal.

Our situation in history is not as unique as we think. Nor is our situation as hopeless as some pessimists think. God said at the conclusion of the Flood of Noah: "I will never again curse the ground because of man, for the imagination of man's heart is evil from his youth; neither will I ever again destroy every living creature as I have done. While the earth remains, seedtime and harvest, cold and heat, summer and winter, day and night, shall not cease" (Gen. 8:21, 22, RSV).

Let us disengage ourselves from a preoccupation with the present moment. Michael Novak reminds us that

under ancient conditions of communications, those who lived in a village, a town . . . or even a country believed

> *they knew "the whole world," . . . For them the destruction of their whole world could descend in one violent sacking, pillaging, and levelling—as more than once, the heads of infants in Israel were dashed against stones, and as Moscow, Kiev, Warsaw fell to Mongol invaders in horrors still not forgotten (the occupation of slavic lands by the Mongols endured for three centuries).*[3]

Half the populations of some countries of Europe were wiped out by black death several centuries ago. So our fears are not unprecedented. It is only that through modern communications the perceived world has enlarged to include most (not quite all) of mankind and nuclear blast with fallout and enduring lethal wastes have added different features to the threatened perils.

At the present time the situation calls for humility of opinion regarding the technical side of the debate about nuclear armament. The latest to the discussion and the least informed seem to say the most. I am, of course, referring to the well-coordinated and apparently well-financed peace movements in Europe and America. There have been several peaks of concern and debate about nuclear arms since 1945. There was one in the mid-fifties and another in 1958. The present one has been developing for several years. Perhaps it will pass. The best explanation for the resurrection of this movement "is the dawning perception that over the last twenty years or so the Soviet Union has radically altered the balance of power through its arms buildup. Coupled with new evidence of Moscow's expansionist tendencies, the inability of even the Carter administration to wring meaningful arms control treaties from the Kremlin and Soviet violations of existing arms treaties, this has created a deep-seated sense of unease."[4]

These fears have been augmented (when they should have been allayed) by efforts of President Ronald Reagan to restore some balance in NATO and U.S. power to the continental power of the Soviets. It seems as though the late thirties and what Churchill called *The Gathering Storm* are here all over again. We are now nearly fifty years removed from the appeasement failures of the thirties. These were climaxed with the tacit approval at Munich, 1938, by Neville Chamberlain, the British prime minister, of Hitler's adventures in central Europe. It was all in the name of "Peace in our Time." Chamberlain came home to the cheers of his countrymen, but Hitler invaded Poland a year later, just the same.

The public, now mildly aroused again, is hearing once more in the peace movement's statements the same arguments that have been around for forty years. It might be well for young people to understand why their elders may be a bit bored by "peace" rhetoric, even though they must respect the opinions and arguments, however stale. Three recent books will help the industrious reader to understand the state and context of nuclear weapons today: *The Wizards of Armageddon* by Fred Kaplan,[5] a young MIT graduate, *The Truth about the Neutron Bomb* by Sam Cohen,[6] the man who invented the neutron bomb, and *Living with Nuclear Weapons* by a study group appointed by Harvard University President Derek Bok[7] to educate the public on the issues of nuclear weapons.

The title *Living with Nuclear Weapons* points in the direction we all will have to take. I submit the following points at least as a calm effort to bring what is both biblical and reasonable to the problem of nuclear war. We cannot "disinvent" the atomic and neutron weapons and the systems which might some day deliver them. My counsel on this question is offered with conviction but with considerable reserve as well. I will heed the advice of the Catholic fathers of Vatican II who, in addressing laymen, said,

> *Often enough the Christian View of things will itself suggest some specific solution in certain circumstances. Yet it happens rather frequently . . . that with equal sincerity some of the faithful will disagree with others on a given matter. Even against the intentions of their proponents, however, solutions proposed on one side or another may be easily confused by many people with the gospel message. Hence it is necessary for people to remember that no one is allowed . . . to appropriate the Church's authority for his opinion. They should always try to enlighten one another . . . preserving mutual charity and caring above all for the common good.*[8]

1. Let us accept the existence of nuclear weapons of unmeasured power for destruction. Former generations could hardly bring enough living offspring to maturity to perpetuate the race. As we have seen, they lived always with scarcity and threat of extinction by wars, plagues, famines, and epidemics. They never lived without evident peril to their existence. In a manner of speaking, "the bomb" has brought us back to "normal"—if life in a fallen world can ever be called normal.

2. Atomic and nuclear weapons have not been detonated in anger for about forty years. This indicates that there is a self-inhibiting feature about their being possessed by several strong powers in the world. The inhibition of use is due, no doubt, to another horrendous reality: the "balance of terror"—each party shrinking from using the bomb, knowing what the terrible consequences would be. There is no guarantee of the future, however; that is why a hot line was set up between the White House and the Kremlin. Yet, an uneasy peace is possible, one in which cordial exchange and commerce could proceed between the powers even under tension. I doubt if Roman Catholic bishops seriously expect their peace-through-persuasion proposals to succeed over the next decades any better than the rude balance of terror of the past forty years. American politics and diplomacy are not sinless by any means, but our leaders are not ruthless gangsters who cynically acknowledge that they keep no promises except convenient ones. The Soviet leadership has been and remains unprincipled, brutal, and ruthless. They are not yet ready to respond to any program of sweet reason.

3. When President Harry Truman directed American planes to drop atomic bombs on Nagasaki and Hiroshima in the summer of 1945, the weapons were employed to end a terrible war, not to start one. Given the determination of the Japanese not to surrender and the requirement of unconditional surrender to which the American forces were committed, there were many more thousands of Japanese and American lives spared, on balance, than if the war had been permitted to grind on. After the detonation of those bombs, everyone was in a mood to lay down arms and to do so quickly. There are millions of us who still remember. It is presumptuous to say that the same mood does not still

prevail, granting similar circumstances. There were costs in life and treasure with the bomb, but the costs would have been greater had the Manhattan Project (the project—authorized by F. D. Roosevelt—which culminated in the production of the atom bomb) never been conceived, especially since Hitler almost beat us to the bomb. There may be, then, as many possibilities for restraint of war as for pursuit of it in nuclear weapons.

4. There have been no world wars since 1945 not only *in spite* of nuclear weapons, but perhaps *on account* of them. The bomb has kept the peace, in the sense of no major war between major powers. Where might the Cuban Bay of Pigs incident of 1962 have gone if there had been no risk of nuclear war? Where might the Soviets have gone in the recent invasion of Afghanistan? It is striking that already the time elapsed between World War II and the present is nearly twice as long as that between the two world wars. The situation in Europe, where both wars started, is no more stable now than then.

5. The possession of nuclear power by one or more contending parties to war tends to reduce the onslaught of an attacking power. If, for example, Syria were attacking Israel, and Israel possessed both nuclear bombs and a dependable delivery system, Syria would stop short of annihilation of Israel or its chief cities precisely because no nation's leaders are likely to allow their very existence to end when use of their nuclear weapons could prevent it. In such a case it would be understood that an attack on Jerusalem or Tel Aviv would mean the annihilation of Damascus.

6. Pacifist advocates of nuclear disarmament (unilateral or bilateral) like to charge that building a nuclear arsenal is a leading cause of poverty. This claim is both implicit and explicit in the Catholic Bishops' Letter of 1983.[9] This is an error, as far as our own country is concerned. Most of the U.S. military budget goes to pay personnel and to maintain pensions for them. According to figures furnished by the budget of the U.S. government for fiscal year 1983, and confirmed by the 1983 report from the Secretary of Defense's office, the 1983 expenditure for nuclear weapons constituted only 9 percent of the military budget. That constitutes 2.9 percent of

the entire federal budget and about 0.6 percent of Gross National Product. Nuclear arms now cost much less than conventional weapons.[10]

In truth, though our country is bound by treaty to defend most of the so-called free world, the total defense budget of the U.S. for 1981 was only 6.1 percent of GNP. That is too much, but is evidently necessary when West Germany—flush against the Soviet armaments—spends only 4.3 percent and Canada 1.7. A comparison shows that "in the free nations, moneys from all sources spent on health, education, welfare and other human purposes exceed moneys spent on weapons by a factor of about 20 to 1."[11] Thus even though we are treaty-bound to bear the burden of defending the Western European democratic republics, all of North America, and Japan, the figures alone demonstrate that armaments are not to be blamed for poverty in our land.

Cutting the expense of government would be beneficial to all nations. Deficit spending by government is commonly acknowledged to cause all kinds of harm to the nations' economies. If, however, our government is to carry out the divine mandate to protect its citizens from its own violence-prone people and to prevent their conquest and enslavement (as well as the conquest of several hundred million good neighbors) by unfriendly nations, then an adequate military is not the point at which to cut the budget.

These are some of the considerations thoughtful Christians will ponder in making up their minds about the unsteady but continuing efforts of the advocates of nuclear pacifism to remove, reduce, or "freeze" nuclear arms from our national defense.

There is much to be said for what is usually called the strategy of deterrence, lately called "peace through strength." The millions of people still alive who were alert to current events in the decade previous to the outbreak of World War II in 1939 cannot help but see how the well-intentioned advocates of unilateral or mutual-but-unverifiable disarmament may be setting us up for World War III against the great Eurasian aggressor, the Soviet Union. Hitler wrote in *Mein Kampf* and elsewhere about his plans to conquer Europe, yet Britain's leadership continued to disarm while Germany armed to the teeth. The actors have now changed, but the delusion is the same.

A full discussion of the moral issues of deterrence would require far more words than this chapter allows. I do assert, nevertheless, that if it is proper for the United States to build up its military in the face of the unparalleled military buildup of the Soviet Union, then to deter attack with nuclear weapons is apparently an inescapable necessity. The Soviets lie to us, they steal our secrets, they break their promises and treaties. God may decide to judge us for our sins anyway, and allow them to defeat us in war and to occupy our land. If this happens, we will know ahead of time that we deserve it. But there is no accredited prophet who can say we should give in to evil greater than our own. Jeremiah is not here to give such counsel; besides, there is still time to repent. Repentance is in order right away. In this, at least, we can agree with the 1983 Pastoral Letter of the American Roman Catholic Bishops.

Two Christian "prophets" of international reputation—Charles Malik and Aleksandr Solzhenitsyn—have spoken to this issue recently. Both of these men of acknowledged piety and wisdom insist that the need of the hour in Christendom is the very opposite of pacifism—philosophical, religious, nuclear or otherwise.

Charles Malik, former Secretary General of the United Nations, is a Christian philosopher and renowned diplomat. In a speech delivered in Washington, D.C. in 1979, he recommended courageous action rather than resignation or submission:

> *He who ponders Deuteronomy and the Psalms, he who meditates in Isaiah and Jeremiah, he who is soaked with the Gospels and Epistles, he who converses daily with David and Paul and Christ, he who knows the deepest spiritual history of the last 2,000 years, he who knows and lives and practices his faith, he who has already tasted the world to come and the power of the Resurrection, how can he fail to devise ways and means for meeting every challenge?*[12]

Malik has frequently commented on the need of the West for Christian renewal and for the recovery of nerve and will to preserve civilization against its declared enemies.

Aleksandr Solzhenitsyn, Russian émigré and author of *The Gulag Archipelago,* has stated repeatedly that our hope to be saved from the oppression of Marxist communism lies in renewal of Christian faith within the leadership and populations of both the Soviet Union and the Christian West. He declares that liberalism has cut our nerve to resist oppression. He has stated this so plainly in the past that he became an embarrassment to Ivy League universities and to two different White House incumbents. In a June 1978 address at Harvard, Solzhenitsyn went so far as to assert:

> *Members of the U.S. antiwar movement wound up [he was reflecting on the Viet Nam antiwar propaganda] being in betrayal of Far Eastern nations, in a genocide and the suffering imposed on 30 million people there. Do those convinced pacifists hear the moans coming from there? Or do they prefer not to hear?*[13]

Solzhenitsyn says, and he ought to know, that

> *communism stops only when it encounters a wall, even if it is only a wall of resolve. The West cannot now avoid erecting such a wall in what is now already its hour of extremity."*[14]

A strong opponent of the peace-church position is Albion W. Knight, a retired brigadier general and United Episcopal minister. In his *Pacifism an Anti-Christian Philosophy,* (Young America's Foundation, 1984) he attempts to prove that pacifism is not only unbiblical, it is antibiblical. Following is a condensation of Knight's impressive summary in answer to the question, "How can the American government build a wall of resolve?"

1. We must recognize the danger we are in. Knight sees, as we do, frightening parallels to the refusal of Britain to see the dangers from Naziism and Hitler right up to the outbreak of

World War II. He mentions the long-term peril of the enlarging alliance with totalitarian, communist China.

2. We must have a moratorium on the disadvantageous arms agreements with the Soviet Union. Though desirable in principle, most such agreements have left us weaker. But the pacifists seem to see arms agreements as the chief road out of our difficulties.

3. Stop helping the enemy. Here Knight refers to loans of money and the exporting of technology to unfriendly nations.

4. Use truth more effectively as weapon: "The Soviet leadership cannot feed its people. We must use truth as a weapon to tell the world what Marxism-Leninism means: poverty and chains. It is an historical fact, not propaganda . . . modernize our radio broadcasting into Iron and Bamboo Curtain countries. We have not done so for fear of being 'provocative.'"

5. We should "move away immediately from the now totally ineffective and grossly immoral doctrine of Mutually Assured Destruction and replace it with the doctrine of Assured Survival." Again Knight quotes Solzhenitsyn: "'This strategy will obviously entail radical conceptual changes and re-thinking of tactics on the part of Western politicians, diplomats and military'" (*Time*, February 18, 1980, p. 25).

Knight goes on to say that national resolve to accomplish such changes will not occur apart from getting our people in right relation to their Maker:

> *We cannot survive unless there is a spiritual reawakening in the land . . . A spiritual reawakening, based upon a firm understanding of our religious roots as written in Holy Scripture, will cause our people to have courage in the face of danger. Pacifism [he is referring to the philosophical doctrine, not Anabaptist nonresistance] leads only to fear and hopelessness. We have more to offer our children and grandchildren than that." (Knight, p. 13)*

Realistic acceptance of the biblical "wars and rumors of wars" and "desolations" determined "to the end" does not require a posture of utter human despair. Twenty years of "American nuclear umbrella" followed by nearly as long with "mutually assured destruction" (MAD) and "balance of terror" cannot be endured forever. Surely there is some form of strategy that does not require the great powers to threaten aggression or propose defense with ever bigger guns, more powerful bombs, and swifter and more elusive projectiles. There is growing conviction and evidence there may be something better, trustworthy and within reach.

President Reagan was thinking along the lines so strongly asserted by Malik and Solzhenitsyn when he said the following over radio and television on March 23, 1983:

> *Let me share with you a vision of the future which offers hope. It is that we embark on a program to counter the awesome Soviet missle threat with measures that are defensive. . . . What if free people could live secure in the knowledge that their security did not rest upon the threat of instant retaliation to deter a Soviet attack; that we could intercept and destroy strategic ballistic missiles [i.e., bombs in rocket-propelled carriers] before they reached our soil or that of our allies? . . .*
>
> *Would it not be better to save lives than to avenge them? . . .*
>
> *My fellow Americans, tonight we are launching an effort which holds the promise of changing human history. There will be risks, and results take time. But with your support, I believe we can do it.*

Advocates of nuclear disarmament of the Western Alliances, whether or not the Soviet Block does the same, have been stridently declaring that there is no defense against nuclear weapons, and there cannot be. They have ridiculed the idea that something might be done, either from the ground or in the atmosphere and space, to keep these explosions from blasting us to pieces, and/or poisoning us with radioactive dust. Now, not only President Reagan but others in position to know are saying that such defensive measures aren't entirely out of the question.

Recently Senator William Armstrong called the usual course of arms discussion up until recently an "intellectual cul-de-sac." He went on to say,

> *From a moral standpoint, our present nuclear doctrine, nuclear destruction, is absolutely bankrupt, because it won't work. . . . It is contrary to several of the main premises of the just-war theory. It does not direct itself to combatants or to keeping civilians safe. . . . Clearly we need something different.*[15]

Senator Armstrong adds that a growing number of scientists and military strategists are advocating a new, purely defensive system. It would operate in space with presently attained skills and means. It would have no offensive capability at all and could be shared safely with any nation on earth, friend or foe. If we could stop ballistic missiles in their flight through space, exploding them high above earth's atmosphere (a good place for all this paraphernalia—the biblical "outer darkness"), then we are safe from them. If our enemies want to feel safe from attack by our missiles, then let them share the technology. In such a case the nuclear space race would be over and everyone could breathe easier.

In 1959 President Dwight D. Eisenhower recognized the advantages of such a system and authorized our military technicians to do research on the feasibility of deploying it. The Department of Defense went to work on it. In less than three years they came up with the conclusion that given six years of lead time they could build such a system and put it in place, with technology then in existence or expected soon to be available.

To those skeptics who wish to regard this as impractical, Buck-Rogers thinking, present advocates of the new project point out that atomic-powered submarines (e.g., the *Polaris*) were delivered only four years after authorization by President Eisenhower and a manned moon landing only seven years after President John F. Kennedy authorized it. They point out that technology for space defense against missiles is already available and tested.

There are several possible defense systems for use in space. The one favored by Senator Armstrong and others in government and in the Department of Defense, is called High Frontier, so named by the privately funded organization that has been working on the system and advising the president.

The system employs no nuclear devices and relies in part upon technology tested by the space shuttle. The project is presently being discussed by the press as well as by committees of Congress.[16]

The High Frontier project is described and defended by retired Lt. General Daniel O. Graham in a small book, *We Must Defend America* (Chicago: Regnery Gateway, 1983). The foreword is by Senator William L. Armstrong. (A paperback edition is available for $2.95 by writing to High Frontier, 1010 Vermont Avenue, Suite 1000, Washington, DC 20005.)

Two new elements have recently been added to the debate about arms limitation and accommodation with the Soviet Union: re-employment of an old lethal weapon of terror—poison gas—and a relatively new one—biological-bacteriological weapons. The latter comes from the ability of science to alter the characteristics of disease-causing microbes (bacteria and viruses) by what is now called genetic engineering. Secretary of Defense Caspar Weinberger first made official comment on Soviet efforts toward creation of "biotechnology" of warfare through creation of lethal viruses in the third annual edition of *Soviet Military Power*. On April 23, 1984, the *Wall Street Journal* began a long series of articles by William Kucewicz entitled "Beyond Yellow Rain." It detailed the results of a seven-month study of the subject.

Kucewicz explains that scientific publications originating in the Soviet Union and by former Soviet scientists now living in the West have opened up extensive, new information on these Soviet advances. According to Kucewicz, the U.S. government is well aware of the chief Soviet centers of research in biochemical warfare and their leading scientists. He writes that "the Soviet Union has placed strong emphasis on development of chemical and biological weapons ever since World War I, when about a half-million Russians fell victim to German gas attacks." Recent employment of poison gas by the Iraqis in their war with Iran appear to be thoroughly verified.

Kucewicz goes on to write, "Afghan freedom-fighters report 'bizarre symptoms—hours long incapacitation, death so sudden it leaves victims frozen in place, rapid decomposition of bodies—that suggest previously unknown chemical agents.'" So, "Genetic engineering seems a natural and almost inevitable next step in the Soviet biochemical weapons program. . . . Normally harmless, non-disease-producing organisms could be modified to . . . produce diseases for which an opponent has no treatment or cure. . . . An aggressor armed with such new biological weapons . . . could vaccinate its own armed forces and population against this new disease, leaving them the only survivors of a worldwide plague." One of the Kucewicz articles quotes Nobel Laureate Joshua Lederberg as saying in a Disarmament Committee address that biological warfare "stands apart from all other devices in the actual threat that it poses to the health and life expectancy of every human being." He warned as long ago as 1970 that biological weapons *"could well become the most efficient means for removing man from the planet."*

But the problem of war with nuclear weapons will not go away just because something even more horrible seems perhaps to have loomed on the far horizon. Every new weapon of the past has been partially neutralized by counter strategies and new defenses. President Reagan supports the idea of effective space-based counter measures against nuclear bombs, missiles, and bomber planes. Lt. Gen. Daniel Graham, whose work in this area has already been mentioned in this chapter, has co-authored with Gregory A. Fossedal, *A Defence That Defends* (Devin-Adair, 180 pages, 1984), a second book advocating this approach. The Soviets may already be working along similar lines. The average American seems to suppose that we must surely already have something of this sort in position, but we do not. In fact, we are party to a treaty with the Soviets (part of SALT I) that prohibits it. In *A Defense That Defends* Daniel Graham and Gregory A. Fossedal contend that we really haven't a choice on whether or not to construct missile defenses; what we must decide is what kind and how quickly.

There clearly will be no end to the perils of residence on this planet nor any reason for God to rescind the biblical obligation for our earthly rulers to be "attending continually upon this very thing" (Rom. 13:6).

We leave the future in the hands of our "merciful Saviour, who with the Father and the Holy Ghost liveth and reigneth one God, world without end."[17]

O Almighty God, the supreme Governor of all things, whose power no creature is able to resist, to whom it belongeth justly to punish sinners and to be merciful to those who truly repent; Save and deliver us, we humbly beseech thee, from the hands of our enemies; that we, being armed with thy defense, may be preserved evermore from all perils, to glorify thee, who art the only giver of victory; through the merits of thy Son, Jesus Christ our Lord. Amen.[18]

NOTES

CHAPTER ONE: To War or Not to War?

1. Roland Bainton, *Christian Attitudes Toward War and Peace* (Nashville: Abingdon, 1960), 216.

CHAPTER TWO: Nonresistance in the Early Church

1. Roland Bainton, "The Early Church and War," *Harvard Theological Review* (July 1946), 190-191.
2. Guy Franklin Herschberger, *War, Peace and Nonresistance* (Scottdale, Penn: Herald Press, 1953), 65.
3. Bainton, "The Early Church," 191.
4. Herschberger, 65-66.
5. Bainton, "The Early Church," 199.
6. Bainton, "The Early Church," 207.
7. *The Fathers of the Church*, vol. 1 (Washington: Catholic University of America, 1962), 260-262.
8. Bainton, "The Early Church," 203.
9. Bainton, "The Early Church," 200-201.
10. E. L. Long, Jr., *War and Conscience in America* (Philadelphia: Westminster, 1968), 54.
11. In addition to the works cited above, several other works treat the views of the early church on war. Those by Protestants are of peace-church persuasion: C. John Cadoux's *The Early Christian Attitude to War* (Sommers, Conn.: Seabury, 1982) is a recent reprint of an old book; Jean-Michel Hornus's *It Is Not Lawful for Me to Fight: Early Christian Attitudes Toward War* (Scottdale, Penn.: Herald Press, 1980), first published in French, is now in English translation. Though carefully researched, Hornus's work is entirely devoted to the apologetics of pacifism; the same may be said of Cadoux's book. Several Roman Catholic authors have written on early Christian pacifism and just-war doctrine; several titles now appear in Paulist Press releases.

CHAPTER THREE: Denizens of the Empire

1. See chapter 9, "Earthen Vessels . . . Exceeding Greatness of Power," in K. S. Latourette, *A History of Christianity,* vol. 1 (New York: Harper and Row, 1975), for discussion of the whole reciprocal effect of church and Empire at this stage, and chapter 6, "The Theory of the Just War in the Christian Roman Empire," in Bainton's *Christian Attitudes,* for the problem of accommodation to war by the church of the time.

CHAPTER FOUR: Peace Thought and the Reformation

1. James M. Stayer's *Anabaptists and the Sword* (Lawrence, Kans.: Coronado Press, 1973) shows this in detail, as does K. S. Latourette's *A History of Christianity* (New York: Harper, 1953), 778-786.

2. Robert D. Culver, *Toward a Biblical View of Civil Government* (Chicago: Moody Press, 1975), 61-83, 274-290.

3. Stayer, *Anabaptist,* 22, 49-69.

4. H. J. Grimm, *The Reformation Era,* 2nd ed. (New York: Macmillan, 1973).

5. Stayer, *Anabaptist,* 68.

6. Contrary to the frequent assertions that Calvin was a sort of dictator in Geneva, he never exercised any power except that of a persuasive pastor-teacher. Let anyone who doubts this read Philip Hughes's *The Register of the Company of Pastors in Geneva in the Time of Calvin* (Grand Rapids: Eerdmans, 1966).

7. Philip Schaff, *The Creeds of Christendom,* vol. III (Grand Rapids: Baker Book House, 1887, 1966), 475-476.

8. Walter Klassen, "Spiritualization in the Reformation," *Mennonite Quarterly Review* (April 1963), 69.

9. Herschberger, 170-206; Herman A. Hoyt, *Then Would My Servants Fight* (Winona Lake, Ind.: Brethren Missionary Herald Co., 1956) 17, 54; John Drescher, "Why Christians Shouldn't Carry Swords," *Christianity Today* (Nov. 7, 1980), 15-23.

10. Daniel Hayes, "The Path of Life," in *Brethren's Tracts and Pamphlets,* vol. 1 (Elgin, Ill.: Brethren Publishing House, 1900), 26-28.

CHAPTER FIVE: Recent Developments

1. Herschberger, *War,* 170-206; Hoyt, *Servants,* 17, 54-69; Drescher, "Why Christians," 15-23.

2. Donald F. Durnbaugh, *The Believers' Church: The History and Character of Radical Protestantism* (New York: Macmillan, 1968) 51-63, 260.

3. Durnbaugh, *The Believers' Church,* 260.

4. *The Brethren Annual of 1943* (Winona Lake, Ind.: Brethren Missionary Herald Co., 1942).

CHAPTER SIX: Tolstoy and the New Breed

1. C. T. H. Wright, librarian and secretary of the London Library, writing in *Encyclopedia Britannica,* 11th ed., s.v. "Leo Tolstoy." This edition of *Britannica* is especially full and accurate in matters pertaining to religious and biblical scholarship. Written at the end of Tolstoy's long life, it is an especially lively essay—far superior to the condensations of it in later editions.

2. Wright, *Britannica.*

3. Durnbaugh, *The Believers' Church*, 238. Cited from an unpublished lecture ("The Church in Mission") delivered by Yoder at the Conference of the Believers' Church, 1967.

4. John Howard Yoder, *The Politics of Jesus* (Grand Rapids: Eerdmans, 1972) 217–218. Yoder calls his own type of pacifism "The Pacifism of the Messianic Community" in his *Nevertheless: Varieties and Shortcomings of Religious Pacifisms*, 2nd ed. (Scottdale, Penn.: Herald Press, 1976), ch. 18.

5. Yoder, *Politics*, 230.

6. Mark O. Hatfield, "Finding the Energy to Continue," *Christianity Today* (Feb. 8, 1980), 23.

7. Jacob J. Enz, *The Christian and Warfare* (Scottdale, Penn.: Herald Press, 1972).

8. Ronald J. Sider, *Rich Christians in an Age of Hunger* (Downers Grove, Ill.: InterVarsity Press), 72–77.

9. Clark Pinnock, "An Evangelical Theology of Liberation," *Sojourners*, (Feb. 1976), 31.

10. Ronald J. Sider, *Christ and Violence* (Scottdale, Penn.: Herald Press, 1979), 52–60.

11. Sider, *Christ and Violence*, 44.

12. Michael Novak, *The Spirit of Democratic Capitalism* (New York: Simon and Schuster, 1982). See also *The Moral Basis of Democratic Capitalism*, three essays by Irving Kristol, Paul Johnson, and Michael Novak (American Enterprise Institute, Washington, D.C., 1980), and *Toward a Theology of the Corporation*, by Michael Novak (American Enterprise Institute, Washington, D.C., 3rd printing, 1982).

13. As quoted by Norman F. Gordon, Jr., *Christian Heritage* (Oct. 1968), 11.

14. Gordon, 11.

15. Gordon, 31.

CHAPTER EIGHT: Wars of the Old Testament

1. Paul M. Mills, *The Bible and War* (Portland, Ore.: Oregon Yearly Meeting of Friends, n.d.), 7.

2. Herman A. Hoyt, *Then Would My Servants Fight* (Winona Lake, Ind.: Brethren Missionary Herald Co., 1956), 74.

3. Hoyt, *Servants*, 71.

4. Hoyt, *Servants*, 72.

5. Hoyt, *Servants*, 72–73.

6. Hoyt, *Servants*, 73–74.

7. Theodore Epp, *Should God's People Partake in War?* (Scottdale, Penn.: Herald Publishing Co., n.d.).

8. Mills, *The Bible*, 9.

9. Millard C. Lind, *Yahweh Is a Warrior: The Theology of Warfare in Ancient Israel*, foreword by Noel Freedman, introduction by J. H. Yoder (Scottdale, Penn.: Herald Press, 1980).

10. Lind, *Yahweh*, 19.

11. Lind, *Yahweh*, 44.

12. Lind, *Yahweh*, 76.

13. I read Lind's book in entirety and found no mention of Numbers 31; nor is it listed in twenty columns of scripture index.

14. See Lind, 56 (*passim*).

15. Culver, *Toward a Biblical View*, 149.

16. Lind, 57.

17. Several other books explain how to defend pacifism in face of apparent evidence to the contrary in the Old Testament. Except for severe limitations on the size of this book I would treat them here. One of these is *The Problem of War in the Old Testament*, by Peter C. Craigie (Grand Rapids: Eerdmans, 1978, 125 pp.). Craigie believes war is always morally evil and that God cannot be both loving and warlike. In an effort to be orthodox, Craigie explains the Old Testament as a sort of historical parable. Another book, Jacob C. Enz's *The Christian and Warfare: The Roots of Pacifism in the Old Testament* (Scottsdale, Penn.: Herald Press, 1972, 95 pp.) does not treat the Old Testament at length. Enz's theology has more affinity with some of the heterodox forms of early Anabaptism than with the theology of the Orthodox Mennonites and Brethren. A third book is *War and Peace from Genesis to Revelation* (Scottdale, Penn.: Herald Press, 1981, 216 pp.), by Vernard Eller. Like several other recent pacifist works, Eller writes from liberal, less-than-orthodox assumptions; hence, he has no adequate view of divine wrath, necessary for a truly biblical understanding of war in the Old Testament. The reader will find excellent reviews of these and several other recent pacifist publications in *The Theology of Christian Resistance*, a symposium edited by Gary North (Tyler, Tex.: Geneva Divinity School Press, 1983, 357 pp.). All of this truly startling book is worthy of wide reading. Many of the chapters support conclusions of the present book.

18. Culver, *Toward a Biblical View*, 182–207.

CHAPTER NINE: The Prince of Peace

1. Drescher, "Why Christians," 15–23.

CHAPTER TEN: Peace Churches and War Powers

1. Hans J. Hillerbrand, "The Anabaptist View of the State" *Mennonite Quarterly Review* 32 (1958), 95–97, as cited in Benjamin Wirt Farley, *John Calvin: Treatises Against the Baptists and Against the Libertines* (Grand Rapids: Baker Book House, 1982), 31.

2. Preaching of the Brethren's nonresistance doctrine in my home church almost invariably would contain a high point which went something like this: "Jesus said, 'Resist not evil'; 'Turn the other cheek'; 'Overcome evil with good'; 'All who take the sword shall perish with the sword.' As long as we have direct commands like these from our Lord, it makes no difference what any biblical saints may or may not have done—we must obey Jesus. There are no passages which take away the plain meaning." This was supposed to end all discussion.

3. Drescher, "Why Christians," 15–16.

4. The Brethren Annual, *The Brethren Evangelist*, vol. 60 (Oct. 29, 1938), 18–19.

5. The Brethren Annual, 1942, *The Brethren Missionary Herald*, vol. 4 (Dec. 26, 1942) quoted in full by Hoyt, 29–33.

6. Dietrich Bonhoeffer states the principles involved in *Ethics*, ed. by Eberhard Bethge (New York: Macmillan, 1955) 303–319.

7. W. Pannenberg, *Ethics*, trans. K. Crim (Philadelphia: Westminster, 1981), 156.

8. Martin Grove Brumbaugh, *A History of the German Baptist Brethren in Europe and America*, 2nd ed. (Elgin, Ill.: Brethren Publishing House, 1899, 1907), 546–548.

9. Durnbaugh, *The Believers' Church*, 260.

10. It is interesting now to see the Jesuits advertising Sider's book in their magazines and apparently joint InterVarsity-Paulist Press production of new publications. Times are changing.

11. If one wishes confirmation of this verdict, consult *Productive Christians in an Age of Guilt Manipulators: A Biblical Response to Ronald Sider* by David Chilton (Tyler, Tex.: Institute for Christian Economics, 1981), especially the introduction, 3-15.

12. Yoder, *Politics,* in chapter 11 equates justification with making peace between different kinds of people, and in chapter 3 proposes that at the heart of Jesus' message was a program of redistribution of goods.

13. C. K. Barrett, in *A Commentary on the Epistle to the Romans* (New York: Harper and Row, 1957) comments on Acts 2:44, 45; 4:34—5:4: "Filled with a sense of their unity as 'brethren,' they instituted a system of partial and voluntary communism. But they carried it out in the economically disastrous way of realizing capital and distributing it as income. . . . no practical steps were taken to replace the capital thus dissipated; and when hard times came, the community had no reserves of any kind." Barrett goes on to say that it then became the burden of Gentile believers elsewhere to support them (p. 230).

CHAPTER ELEVEN: The Christian's Social Responsibility

1. Werner Elert, *The Christian Ethos: The Foundations of the Christian Way of Life* (Philadelphia: Fortress Press, 1957), 119.

2. Elert, *Ethos,* 79.

3. Elert, *Ethos,* 79.

4. Albion W. Knight, Jr. and Frederick D. Wilhelmsen, *Pacifism an Anti-Christian Philosophy* (Reston, Va.: Young Americas Foundation, 1984).

CHAPTER TWELVE: Christian Witness to the State about War

1. I have discussed this at length elsewhere. See *Toward a Biblical View of Civil Government,* 61-80.

2. These are the proposals of (1) Thomas Aquinas, George Hegel, and their disciples; (2) John Locke, Thomas Hobbes, and Jean Jacques Rousseau; and (3) Karl Marx, Lenin, and Marxian socialism (Soviet communism).

3. As summarized by Jachem Douma, "The Ethical Justification of Deterrence," *Reformed Perspective* (May 1982), 8.

4. J. G. Davies, *Christians, Politics and Violent Revolution* (Maryknoll, N.Y.: Orbis Books, 1976), 166-167.

5. Saint Augustine, *City of God,* XIX, 12.

6. *City of God,* XIX, 7.

7. Saint Thomas Aquinas, *Summa Theologica,* part II-II, question 40, article 1.

8. A. A. Hodge, *The Confession of Faith: A Handbook of Christian Doctrine Expounding the Westminster Confession* (London: Banner of Truth, reprint 1964), 296.

9. For a more complete understanding of the just-war positions, the reader would do well to consult *The Wars of America* (Grand Rapids: Eerdmans, 1981), edited by Ronald A. Wells, a professor of history at Calvin College. In eight essays—each by a professional evangelical historian—this book attempts to assess the ethics of the wars of America. Assuming at least relative validity to traditional Christian just-war criteria, the authors assess each of America's wars to discern whether or not any or all of them may rightly be called just wars. The War of 1812, the Mexican War, the war

with Spain, and the Viet Nam War are judged severely by the authors. The editor summarizes near the end: "Most of the writers of this book accept the notion that our Christian commitment requires us to be active in society, and that we accept, however reluctantly, the notion that coercive force must be allowed. Philosophically, at least, we accept the notion of 'just war,' . . . While allowing for the philosophical plausibility of 'just war,' however, we are not generally convinced that America's wars have been just merely because Americans have claimed they were" (p. 210).

CHAPTER THIRTEEN: Nuclear "Pacifism"

1. Thomas Bray, "Perspectives on the Nuclear Know-Nothings," *Wall Street Journal* (July 6, 1983).

2. Michael Novak, "Moral Clarity in the Nuclear Age," *Catholicism in Crisis* (March, 1983), paragraph 4.

3. Novak, "Moral Clarity," paragraph 9.

4. Bray, "Perspectives."

5. Fred Kaplan, *The Wizards of Armageddon* (New York: Simon and Schuster, 1983, 452 pages).

6. Sam Cohen, *The Truth about the Neutron Bomb* (Morrow, 1983, 226 pages).

7. *Living with the Neutron Bomb* (Cambridge, Mass.: Harvard University Press/Bantam, 1983, 268 pages).

8. *The Documents of Vatican II* (New York: Guild Press, 1966), 244.

9. This carefully worded "pastoral letter" of book length, prepared by bishops of the United States Roman Catholic hierarchy, was published under the title "The Challenge of Peace: God's Promise and Our Response" as a special supplement to *The Catholic Bulletin* (May 26, 1983). It is available for $1.00 at the various diocesan offices.

10. Novak, "Perspectives," paragraph 34 provides these figures and documents them.

11. Novak, "Perspectives," paragraph 35.

12. *Congressional Record* (April 5, 1979), p.S. 4082, as cited by Knight, Wilhelmsen, *Pacifism*, 13.

13. *Washington Post* (June 11, 1978), as quoted by Knight, Wilhelmsen, *Pacifism*, 11–12.

14. *Time* (Feb. 18, 1980), as cited by Knight, Wilhelmsen, *Pacifism*, 24.

15. "Bill Armstrong, Senator and Christian," *Christianity Today*, (Nov. 11, 1983).

16. Most of us have too many things to do to spend large amounts of time keeping up with the technical problems of war preparation in the nuclear age, to say nothing of the debate about how to control or eliminate nuclear weapons. So it likely has escaped the notice of most readers that in 1972 a very unlikely appearing agreement was made between the U.S. and the Soviets. The agreement outlawed any defense at all against ballistic missiles (it was called the ABM Treaty). Why? The idea seems to be that if neither nation could keep the other's intercontinental nuclear missiles from striking, fear of retaliation would keep both sides from ever using their missiles. This is part of the "balance of terror" we read about, and of mutually-assured destruction (MAD). The result has been "proliferation" and stepped-up production of weapons. The possibility of defense against these missiles is supposed to make the "unthinkable" conflict with nuclear weapons "thinkable." Defense systems against these intercontinental missiles is therefore undesirable, we are told. This is probably the first time in

history that defensive preparations have been regarded as prelude to general destruction.

17. *The Book of Common Prayer,* "Prayer for Children."
18. *The Book of Common Prayer,* "Prayer in Time of War and Tumult."

FOR FURTHER READING

If you should want to pursue a thorough study of the subject of war, nonresistance, pacifism, or the threat of nuclear holocaust, I would recommend that you consult the bibliography of the book *War: Four Christian Views,* edited by Robert G. Clouse (Downers Grove, Ill.: InterVarsity Press, 1981, pp. 201–208). Clouse supplies 112 titles of recent and classical works, with very fair and informative annotations to each. These titles balance the picture by referring the reader to many different points of view, including several secular approaches.

If you are interested in books defending pacifism from the new peace-church "pacifist activism" viewpoint, I would suggest that you direct an inquiry to Herald Press (616 Walnut Ave., Scottdale, Penn. 15683), the leading Mennonite publisher in America. Herald Press publishes *Peace Shelf,* a periodically-updated list of recent books and other materials on the subject.

Most bibliographies of literature advocating some form of just-war doctrine appear not in books but in pamphlets, brochures, and privately-distributed materials not readily available. To receive information on some of the best books written from Roman Catholic just-war perspectives, I would encourage you to get on the mailing list of Fr. William O'Brien, through Newman Press (Westminster, Penn.)

Finally, I would strongly urge all readers interested in the subject of this book to subscribe to the *Wall Street Journal* and read—daily—the editorial page and book review section.

—Robert Duncan Culver